"*The Pursuit of Perfect* drew me in immediately and kept me captivated for hours. Tal Ben-Shahar seamlessly weaves personal examples, Gladwellian stories, and illuminating research findings to impart a valuable message. Every person concerned with success—and that includes most of us—should read this book."

—*Sonja Lyubomirsky, author of* The How of Happiness

"This book will inspire you to realize your innate potential for happiness and awaken the genuine aspiration to change, while avoiding the trap of perfectionism and the unrealistic demands of the ego."

—*Matthieu Ricard, author of* Happiness: A Guide to Developing Life's Most Important Skill

"Tal Ben-Shahar has done it again! In *Happier*, he invited us to rethink our assumptions about happiness and what it depends on. Now, in *The Pursuit of Perfect*, he invites us to discard the fallacy that the pursuit of 'perfect' is the best indicator of success and happiness."

—*Nathaniel Branden,*
*author of* The Six Pillars of Self-Esteem

*the*

*Pursuit*

*of*

# PERFECT

## How to Stop Chasing Perfection and Start Living a *RICHER, HAPPIER* Life

## *TAL BEN-SHAHAR, Ph.D.*

New York   Chicago   San Francisco   Lisbon   London   Madrid   Mexico City
Milan   New Delhi   San Juan   Seoul   Singapore   Sydney   Toronto

*The McGraw-Hill Companies*

**Library of Congress Cataloging-in-Publication Data**

Ben-Shahar, Tal.
   The pursuit of perfect : how to stop chasing and start living a richer, happier
life / by Tal Ben-Shahar.
        p.    cm.
   Includes bibliographical references.
   ISBN 978-0-07-160882-4 (alk. paper)
   1. Success.    2. Happiness.    I. Title.

BF637.S8B446    2009
155.2′32—dc22                                           2008053219

1  2  3  4  5  6  7  8  9  10  11  12  13  14  15  16  17  18  19  20  21  22  23    FGR/FGR    0  9

ISBN 978-0-07-160882-4
MHID     0-07-160882-6

Detail from Raphael's *The School of Athens*, p. 92: Photo by Time Life Pictures/
Mansell/Time Life Pictures/Getty Images

McGraw-Hill books are available at special quantity discounts to use as premiums and
sales promotions or for use in corporate training programs. To contact a representative,
please visit the Contact Us pages at www.mhprofessional.com.

This book is printed on acid-free paper.

*To Tami, my love*

# Contents

# Preface

For the last decade I have been teaching happiness. As is true for many people teaching at universities, what first began as a subject of great personal interest to me eventually became the subject of my academic research. I started thinking about happiness as a successful but unhappy student, following several years as a successful but unhappy professional athlete. My desire to understand the cause of my unhappiness led me into the then-emerging field of positive psychology. Unlike traditional psychology, which mostly focuses on neurosis, depression, and anxiety, positive psychology focuses on the conditions that lead people, organizations, and communities to flourish. Simply put, positive psychology is the science of happiness.

I benefited a great deal from my studies of positive psychology and wanted to share what I had learned with others. I always knew, of course, that people were interested in the subject of happiness, but I never expected interest on the scale that I encountered when I began to write and lecture on how to lead a more meaningful and pleasurable life.

In letters from readers, conversations with my undergraduate students, and discussions in my seminars—whether with entrepreneurs in Shanghai, political leaders in Canberra, at-risk teenagers in New York, journalists in Cape Town, or teachers in Paris—I saw how passionately committed people were to improving their own lives and increasing the well-being of their communities. Over time, I began to see that all these diverse groups shared more than just an interest in leading happier lives—they also shared some of the major obstacles to becoming happier. One of those obstacles, arguably the number one obstacle, is the aspiration to a life that is not just happier but *perfect*.

This became apparent to me through two recurring, and somewhat surprising, reactions I encountered during conversations about happiness. First, people would often say that they weren't happy; but as they described their lives and their feelings in greater detail, it became clear that what they really meant was that they weren't happy *all the time*. Second, people would comment that I myself didn't seem to be bursting with joy as, they thought, a "happiness expert" ought to be at every moment. And when I would talk about my failures or my fears, they would express surprise that I considered myself happy despite such undesirable experiences. Underlying both of these reactions is the assumption that truly happy people are somehow immune from feeling sadness, fear, and anxiety or from experiencing failures and setbacks in life. The pervasiveness of this assumption—across generations, continents, and cultures—made me realize something astounding: I was surrounded by Perfectionists.

I had for some time considered myself a recovering Perfectionist but had never before understood the phenomenon of perfectionism to be so pervasive. Many of the people I met and heard from, whom I recognized as fellow Perfectionists, may not have described themselves—or been seen by others—as such. Yet to greater or lesser degrees their assumptions, their ways of thinking and being, were precisely those that define Perfectionists. Moreover, they were all, in one way or another, suffering the harmful consequences of perfectionism.

This book is about what perfectionism really is and about how to overcome this obstacle to a happier life. Like my previous book, *Happier*, this book too was written as a workbook. To benefit from it in a meaningful way, readers should not read straight through as if reading a novel. Instead, I suggest reading this book slowly, with stops and starts, taking time to apply the material and to reflect on it. To help you with this process of action and reflection, there are exercises at the end of each chapter. Throughout the book, there are also Time-Ins— questions or ideas to consider. They provide an occasion to pause and reflect—and therefore to better understand and assimilate the material. The exercises and Time-Ins can be done alone, in pairs, or in groups. The book can provide material for book clubs interested in personal development, as well as for couples wishing to cultivate greater intimacy.

# Acknowledgments

For a person with perfectionist tendencies, writing the acknowledgments section of a book is particularly difficult. A perfect section would mention everyone who has contributed, directly or indirectly, to this book. Given the impossibility of thanking every person to whom I am indebted, I will put into practice the ideas in this book and settle for something that is "good enough," which unfortunately means leaving out many names. My apologies and my gratitude to all of them.

Kim Cooper, my dear friend and brilliant teacher, provided invaluable assistance on drafts of this book. Throughout the process, she has helped me sharpen my thinking and hone my writing.

Katy Aisenberg's insights found their way into the book—and into my life—with much grace and compassion. Zvia Sarel's support, emotionally and intellectually, has been immeasurable.

My friends, colleagues, and students at the Interdisciplinary Center in Herzliya, Israel, provided me the kind of work environment that hitherto I had only read about.

I am grateful to Idan Ofer for believing in me and for providing me the opportunities to fail and learn. My appreciation to

Rami Ziv, friend and teacher, who, when I was sixteen, planted the seed that grew into my understanding of the "permission to be human." Ohad Kamin has for the last decade inspired me to write and think and experience. My friends and colleagues Jan Elsner, Barbara Heilemann, and Amanda Horne further my thinking each time we meet. Adam Vital closely read and insightfully commented on the manuscript.

I have been fortunate to work with C. J. Lonoff from Speaking Matters and am grateful for her professionalism, and for truly caring. My deep gratitude to John Aherne and Ann Pryor from McGraw-Hill for their invaluable help and for making business a pleasure. To Rafe Sagalyn, Bridget Wagner, Jennifer Graham Redd, and Shannon O'Neill from the Sagalyn Agency: what would I have done without you?

No words can express my gratitude to my family—parents, siblings, children, and other relatives—who never allowed me to forget, no matter how immersed I was in my work, what life is truly about.

This book is dedicated to Tami, my wife and role model, who shows me every day that the optimal love I write about in this book actually exists.

# Introduction

In the depth of winter, I finally learned that there was within me an invincible summer.

—*Albert Camus*

t was mid-January. I saw nothing around me as I cut across Harvard Yard toward the austere psychology building on the other side of campus. Once there, I stood before my professor's closed door. I raised my eyes and scanned the ID numbers on the grade sheet, column by column, and then straight across the page, finding it difficult to see clearly what was in front of me. Once again, my anxiety had rendered me nearly blind.

My first two years of college had been unhappy. I always felt that the sword of Damocles was hanging over my head. What if I missed a crucial word during a lecture? What if I was caught off guard during a seminar and was unable to answer the professor's question? What if I didn't have a chance to proofread my paper for a third and final time before submitting it? Any of these situations could lead to an imperfect performance, to failure, and to the end of the possibility of becoming the kind of person and attaining the kind of life that I envisioned for myself.

That day, standing at my professor's door, one of my great fears materialized. I failed to get an A. I rushed back to my room and locked the door behind me.

Nobody likes to fail, but there is a difference between a normal aversion to failure and an intense fear of failure. Aversion to failure motivates us to take necessary precautions and to work harder to achieve success. By contrast, intense fear of failure often handicaps us, making us reject failure so vigorously that we cannot take the risks that are necessary for growth. This fear not only compromises our performance but jeopardizes our overall psychological well-being.

Failure is an inescapable part of life and a critically important part of any successful life. We learn to walk by falling, to talk by babbling, to shoot a basket by missing, and to color the inside of a square by scribbling outside the box. Those who intensely fear failing end up falling short of their potential. *We either learn to fail or we fail to learn.*

Ten years later I was eating lunch in the dining hall of Leverett House, one of Harvard's undergraduate dorms. It was October, the fall semester was in progress, and most of the leaves outside the window had turned glaring orange, red, and yellow. The most interesting ones to me were those that seemed still to be struggling to let nature take its course and turn those brighter hues.

"May I join you?" Matt, a senior, asked. My mouth was full, so I nodded and smiled. "I hear you're teaching a class on happiness," Matt said, as he sat down opposite me.

"That's right, it's about positive psychology," I responded, eager to tell him all about my new course.

But before I could continue, Matt jumped in. "You know, my roommate Steve is taking your class, so you'd better watch out."

"Watch out? Why?" I asked, expecting him to divulge some dark secret about Steve.

"Because," he replied, "if I ever see you looking unhappy, I'm going to tell him."

Matt was clearly joking—or, at least half joking. The assumption underlying his remark, though, was a serious—and a common—one: that a happy life is composed of an endless stream of positive emotions and that a person who experiences envy or anger, disappointment or sadness, fear or anxiety is not *really* happy. But in fact, the only people who don't experience these normal unpleasant feelings are psychopaths. And the dead. Experiencing these emotions, at times, is actually a good sign—a sign that we are most likely not psychopathic and that we are most certainly alive.

Paradoxically, when we do not allow ourselves to experience painful emotions, we limit our capacity for happiness. All our feelings flow along the same emotional pipeline, so when we block painful emotions, we are also indirectly blocking pleasurable ones. And these painful emotions only expand and intensify when they aren't released. When they finally break through—and they eventually do break through in one way or another—they overwhelm us.

Painful emotions are an inevitable part of the experience of being human, and therefore rejecting them is ultimately rejecting part of our humanity. To lead a full and fulfilling life—a *happy* life—we need to allow ourselves to experience the full range of human emotions. In other words, *we need to give ourselves the permission to be human.*

Alasdaire Clayre's life seemed perfect. He was a star student at Oxford University and later became one of its most celebrated scholars, winning accolades, awards, and fellowships. Not one to restrict himself to the ivory tower, he published a novel and a collection of poems and recorded two albums that included some of his own compositions. He then wrote, directed, produced, and presented *The Heart of the Dragon*, a twelve-part television series on China.

The series won an Emmy Award, but Clayre was not there to receive it. At the age of forty-eight, shortly after completing the series, Clayre committed suicide by jumping in front of a moving train.

Would knowing that he was about to win the Emmy have made any difference? His ex-wife says that "the Emmy was a symbol of success that would have meant a great deal to him, that would have given him self-esteem." But, she adds, "he had so many symbols of success much grander than the Emmy" and none of them satisfied him: "he needed a new one each time he did something."[1]

Ultimately, Clayre never considered anything he did to be good enough. Although he was clearly a great success, he was unable to see himself as successful. He actually rejected success. First, he consistently measured himself against standards that were almost impossible to meet. Second, even when he attained the near impossible, he would quickly dismiss his success as trivial and move on to the next impossible dream.

The desire for success is part of our nature. And many of us are driven to reach greater and greater heights, which can lead to personal success and societal progress. Great expectations can indeed lead to great rewards. However, to lead a life that is both successful and fulfilling, our standards of success must be *realistic*, and we must be able to enjoy, and be grateful for, our achievements. *We need to ground our dreams in reality and appreciate our accomplishments.*

These three stories—my extreme anxiety over a less-than-perfect grade, Matt's warning that I had better seem happy all the time, and the tragedy of Clayre's inability to enjoy success—capture three distinct yet interrelated aspects of perfectionism: rejection of *failure*, rejection of *painful emotions*, and rejection of *success*. We see the negative effects of these aspects of perfectionism all around us and often within us.

We see intense fear of failure in schoolchildren who do not venture outside the box, who stop experimenting, and who thus diminish their ability to learn and to grow. We see it in college students who become chronic procrastinators, afraid to begin a project if they are not certain of a perfect outcome. We see it in the workplace, where innovation is sacrificed on the altar of the tried-and-true, the safe—and the mediocre.

Behaviors like these are not the only manifestations of intense fear of failure. Sometimes we turn this fear inward. We all know people who seem perennially cheerful even in the face of major disappointments, who are relentlessly optimistic regardless of objective reality, who bounce back quickly and seem emotionally unscathed following real traumas and tragedies. While a positive attitude and resilience clearly contribute to well-being, rejecting painful emotions because there is no room for them in our idealized vision of a happy life is unhealthy in the long run. Taking emotional shortcuts—detouring to avoid certain feelings—can, paradoxically, diminish happiness.

It's easy to understand how perfectionism leads to the rejection of failure and painful emotions. What is surprising, though, is how perfectionism can lead to the rejection of *success*. We see this in people who seem to "have it all" but are nevertheless unhappy. If the only dream we have is of a perfect life, we are doomed to disappointment since such dreams simply cannot come true in the real world. It was Clayre's intense perfectionism that made all of his real-life accomplishments seem trivial to him and made him unable to take real and lasting pleasure in his successes.

**TIME-IN** Can you recognize yourself or someone you know in one of the three stories?

For a long time, perfectionism was considered by psychologists as a kind of neurosis. In 1980 psychologist David Burns described Perfectionists as "those whose standards are high beyond reach or reason, people who strain compulsively and unremittingly toward impossible goals and who measure their own worth entirely in terms of productivity and accomplishment."[2] Recently, psychologists have begun to see perfectionism as more complex and have begun to explore the ways in which it may not be purely negative. Indeed, they have found that perfectionism can be beneficial in some ways, driving people to work hard and set high personal standards.

In light of this, psychologists today differentiate between positive perfectionism, which is adaptive and healthy, and negative perfectionism, which is maladaptive and neurotic.[3] I regard these two types of perfectionism as so dramatically different in both their underlying nature and their ramifications that I prefer to use entirely different terms to refer to them. Throughout this book, I will refer to negative perfectionism simply as *perfectionism* and to positive perfectionism as *optimalism*.[4]

The Oxford English Dictionary defines *optimal* as the "best, most favorable, especially under a particular set of circumstances." Finding the optimal—whether it is the best use of the limited time we have in a day (or in our lives) or the best house we can buy given our budget—is something we are all actually accustomed to doing. We acknowledge the *constraints* of reality—that there are only twenty-four hours in a day, that we have a limited amount of money to spend—and we arrange our lives accordingly.

The researchers who introduced the concept of positive psychology described it as "the scientific study of *optimal* human functioning."[5] They understood that there are inherent limitations to being human, that we all must make trade-offs in life, and that no one can have it all. The fundamental question that positive psychology asks is the following: what is the *best possible life* that we can live? In this sense, positive psychology, with its focus on the optimal, is quite different from much of what we find in the self-help movement, which so often invites us to imagine and aspire to living a perfect life. That aspiration, paradoxically, can lead to a great deal of frustration and unhappiness.

The key difference between the Perfectionist and the Optimalist is that the former essentially *rejects* reality while the latter *accepts* it. We will explore this important distinction later, but for now we can see this difference in the way each perceives and reacts to failure, painful emotions, and success.

The Perfectionist expects her path toward any goal—and, indeed, her entire journey through life—to be direct, smooth, and free of obstacles. When, inevitably, it isn't—when, for instance, she fails at a task, or when things don't quite turn out the way she expected—she is extremely frustrated and has difficulty coping. While the Perfectionist *rejects failure*, the Optimalist *accepts* it as a natural part of life and as an experience that is inextricably linked to success. She understands that failure to get the job she wanted or arguing with her spouse is part of a full and fulfilling life; she learns what she can from these experiences and emerges stronger and more resilient. I was unhappy in college, in large part because I could not accept failure as a necessary part of learning—and of living.

The Perfectionist believes that a happy life comprises an uninterrupted stream of positive emotions. And because he, of course, aspires to be happy, he *rejects painful emotions*. He denies himself the permission to feel sad when a work opportunity is lost or to experience the deep pain that follows the dissolution of a meaningful relationship. The Optimalist, on the other hand, *accepts* that painful emotions are an inevitable part of being alive. He gives room for sadness and pain, allowing such feelings to deepen his overall experience of life—the unpleasant as well as the pleasant. Matt, the student who jokingly threatened to report me to his roommate if he saw me unhappy, thought that a person teaching happiness should radiate joy 24-7. Matt's idea was not only unrealistic, it was in fact a recipe for unhappiness.

The Perfectionist is never satisfied. She consistently sets goals and standards that are for all intents and purposes impossible to meet, thereby from the outset *rejecting the possibility of success*. No matter what she achieves—how well she does in school or how high up the work ladder she climbs—she can never take any pleasure in her accomplishments. No matter what she has—how much money she has made, how wonderful her spouse is, how much recognition she receives from her peers—it is never good enough for her. What she is actually doing is rejecting success from her life, because regardless of her *objective* successes, she never *feels* successful. The Optimalist also sets extremely high standards, but her standards are attainable because they are grounded in reality. When she meets her goals, she appreciates her successes and takes time to experience gratitude for her accomplishments. In this sense, what differentiates the Optimalist from the Perfectionist is the Optimalist's *acceptance* of reality. When the Optimalist reaches her goals, she feels real satisfaction and real pleasure in her success. Clayre desperately chased success throughout his life, but because his view of what success meant was unrealistic, he could never succeed (in his terms) and thus could never be happy.

Perfectionists *reject reality* and replace it with a fantasy world—a world in which there is no failure and no painful emotions and in which their standards for success, no matter how unrealistic, can actually be met. Optimalists *accept reality*—they accept that in the real world some failure and sorrow is inevitable and that success has to be measured against standards that are actually attainable.

Perfectionists pay an extremely high emotional price for rejecting reality. Their rejection of failure leads to anxiety, because the possibility that they may fail is always there. Their rejection of painful emotions often leads to an intensification of the very emotion they are trying to suppress, ultimately leading to even more pain. Their rejection of real-world limits and constraints leads them to set unreasonable and unattainable standards for success, and because they can never meet these standards, they are constantly plagued by feelings of frustration and inadequacy.

Optimalists, on the other hand, derive great emotional benefit, and are able to lead rich and fulfilling lives, by accepting reality. Because they accept failure as natural—even if they do not *enjoy* failing—they experience less performance anxiety and derive more enjoyment from their activities. Because they accept painful emotions as an inevitable part of being alive, they do not exacerbate them by trying to suppress them—they experience them, learn from them, and move on. Because they accept real-world limits and constraints, they set goals that they can actually attain and are thus able to experience, appreciate, and enjoy success.

| Perfectionist | Optimalist |
|---|---|
| Rejects failure | Accepts failure |
| Rejects painful emotions | Accepts painful emotions |
| Rejects success | Accepts success |
| *Rejects reality* | *Accepts reality* |

In essence, Perfectionists reject everything that deviates from their flawless, faultless ideal vision, and as a result they suffer whenever they do not meet their own unrealistic standards. Optimalists accept, and make the best of, everything that life has to offer.

**TIME-IN** Are there particular areas in your life where you tend to be an Optimalist? Are there areas in which you are more of a Perfectionist?

The book is divided into three parts. In Part 1, I lay out the theory of perfectionism, developing the ideas that I introduced above. Chapter 1 deals with the importance of accepting failure and the idea that we need to learn to fail or else we will fail to learn. Chapter 2 deals with accepting emotions and develops the idea that we need to give ourselves permission to be human. Chapter 3 is about accepting success, about the importance of setting ambitious yet realistic goals and then appreciating our success in achieving them. The final chapter of this part of the book is about accepting reality, which is the basis for countering perfectionist tendencies.

In the second part of the book, I apply ideas from the first part to specific areas. Chapter 5 discusses what teachers and parents can do to help children attain both happiness and success. Chapter 6 takes perfectionism and optimalism to the workplace, showing the benefits of being an Optimalist. In Chapter 7, I argue that attaining true love entails giving up unrealistic notions of perfect love.

The third and final part of the book contains a series of short meditations, each on a different aspect of perfectionism. The first meditation explores why it is often so difficult to change our attitudes and behaviors, specifically when it comes to our perfectionist tendencies. The second meditation introduces a cognitive therapeutic technique that can be used to deal with perfectionism.

In the third meditation, I offer some advice on giving advice to others. The fourth meditation looks at the proper place of psychiatric medication in dealing with psychological disease. The fifth meditation explores the role of suffering in our lives. The sixth meditation underscores the importance of self-love, and the seventh meditation explores how perfectionism taints our treatment of others. The pro-aging movement—as opposed to the anti-aging movement—is the subject of the eighth meditation. The ninth meditation discusses the "great deception" and the price people pay for hiding their emotions. The final meditation is on the limits of knowing and our acceptance of not knowing.

Of all the topics that I write about or teach, the subject of perfectionism is closest to my heart and mind because I have had to face my own destructive perfectionist tendencies. Given that this has always been such a personally meaningful topic to me, it came as no surprise that my students often remarked that the lectures on perfectionism were the most meaningful ones to them too. As Carl Rogers once wrote, "What is most personal is most general."[6]

My hope is that this book is as meaningful to you as writing it has been to me and as the topic has been for my students. Throughout the book, I share many personal anecdotes as well as stories about other people; I hope they will bring to life the rigorous research and the scientific evidence that form the foundation of this book.

Part 1

# The
# THEORY

# 1

# Accepting Failure

---

**The greatest mistake a man can make is to be afraid of making one.**

*—Elbert Hubbard*

O n the evening of May 31, 1987, I became Israel's youngest-ever national squash champion. I was thrilled to win the championship and felt truly happy. For about three hours. And then I began to think that this accomplishment wasn't actually very significant: squash, after all, was not a major sport in Israel, and there were only a few thousand players. Was it really a big deal to be the best of such a small group? By the next morning I decided that the deep and lasting satisfaction I craved would only come if I won a world championship. I resolved right then to become the best player in the world. A few weeks later I graduated from high school, packed my bags, and left for England, which was considered the center of international squash. From Heathrow Airport, I took the underground train straight to Stripes, the squash club in Ealing Broadway where the world champion, Jansher Khan, trained. And although he did not know it, that was the day I started my apprenticeship with him.

I followed his every move on the court, in the gym, and on the road. Each morning before heading to the club, he ran seven miles; so I did the same. He then spent four hours on court, playing against a few training partners and working out with his coach; so I did the same. In the afternoon he lifted weights for an hour and then stretched for another hour; so I did the same.

The first step in my plan to win the world championship was to improve quickly, so that Jansher would invite me to be one of his regular training partners. I did in fact improve, and within six months of moving to England, I was invited by Jansher to play with him whenever one of his regular partners could not make it. A few months later I became one of the regulars. Jansher and I played and trained together every day, and when he traveled to tournaments I would join him and either warm up with him before his match or, if the match was not taxing for him (and most matches weren't), we would play afterward.

Although I improved by leaps and bounds, there was a price. While Jansher had gradually built up to the intensity of his workout regime, I had taken a shortcut. When I arrived in England, I believed I had only two options before me: either to train like the world champion (and become one myself) or not to train at all (and give up on my dream). All or nothing. The intensity of Jansher's regime far exceeded anything I had ever done before. No matter, I thought: to be a world champion, do as the world champion does.

My body thought differently. I began to get injured with increasing regularity. Initially, the injuries were minor—a pulled hamstring, mild backache, soreness in my knee—nothing that could keep me off the court for more than a couple of days. And I felt confident in my approach, because despite my injuries, I was training the way the world champion trained, and my game continued to improve.

But I was dismayed to find that my performance was much weaker in tournaments than during practice. While I had no problem focusing for hours at a time during practice sessions, intense pre-match jitters kept me awake at night and hurt my performance on the court. Playing the big matches or the big points, I would often choke under the pressure.

A year after moving to London, I reached the final of a major junior tournament. I was expected to win comfortably, having beaten the top ranked players in earlier rounds. My coach was watching, my friends were rooting for me, and a reporter from the local paper was there, ready to let the world know about the bright new star on the squash circuit. I won the first two games easily and was within two points of clinching the match when first my feet, then my leg, and finally my arm cramped. I lost the match.

I had never experienced such cramps during practice, no matter how hard I had trained, and it was clear to me that the physical symptoms were a result of psychological pressure. What held me back on that occasion, and on so many other occasions, was my intense fear of failure. In my quest to become the world champion, failure was not an option. By this I mean that not only did I regard becoming the world champion the only goal worth attaining, but I also believed that only the shortest and most direct route to my goal was acceptable. The road to the top had to be a straight line—there was no time (and, I believed, no reason) for anything else.

But my body, once again, thought otherwise. After two years of doing too much too soon, the injuries gradually became more serious, taking weeks rather than days to heal. Nevertheless, I stuck to my punishing regime. Eventually, at the grand old age of twenty-one, plagued by injuries and strongly advised by medical experts to slow down, I had to give up my dream of becoming the best player in the world. I was devastated, and yet part of me felt relieved: the doctors had provided me with an acceptable excuse for my failure.

As an alternative to a professional athletic career, I applied to college. My focus shifted from sports to academia. But I brought to the classroom the same behaviors, feelings, and attitudes that had driven me on the court. Once again, I believed that I faced a choice of all or nothing, in terms of how much work I needed to do and what kind of grades I had to earn. And so I applied myself to reading every word that every professor assigned, and I tolerated nothing short of perfect grades on all the papers that I wrote and the exams that I took. Working to achieve this goal kept me up at night, and anxiety that I still might fail kept me up long after all the papers were handed in and the exams were taken. As a result, I spent my first years of college in a state of almost constant stress and unhappiness.

**TIME-IN** Can you relate to the preceding story? In what ways? Do you know others who have been through, or are going through, similar experiences?

My original plan, when I entered college, was to major in one of the hard sciences. My best grades had always been in science and mathematics. To me, that was reason enough to continue along the same path; it was the most straightforward way to achieve perfect grades. But although I did very well in my courses, my unhappiness and my increasing weariness gradually drew me away from this safe choice, and I began to explore the humanities and social sciences. I was initially uneasy about leaving the hard sciences, with their satisfying, objective truths, and was unsure about the more nuanced—and to me, uncharted—territory of the "softer" disciplines. However, my desire to alleviate the anxiety and unhappiness was stronger than my fear and uneasiness about change, and so at the beginning of my junior year I switched my major from computer science to psychology and philosophy.

It was then that I encountered for the first time the research on perfectionism conducted by David Burns, Randy Frost, Gordon Flett, and Paul Hewitt. I had not realized until then that so many people struggled, to a greater or lesser degree, with the same problems I had. Both the research and the knowledge that I was not alone comforted me somewhat. Initially, I scanned the literature looking for a quick fix to get me from where I was (a maladaptive Perfectionist) to where I wanted to be (an adaptive Perfectionist)—I was still looking for the straight-line solution. But when my attempts failed, I delved deeper into the research, and over time I gained a deeper understanding of the subject, and of myself.

## Perfectionism Versus Optimalism

Let's take a look at the essential differences between the Perfectionist, who rejects failure, and the Optimalist, who accepts it. First, though, it is important to understand that perfectionism and optimalism are not distinct qualities that are entirely independent of each other. No person is 100 percent a Perfectionist or 100 percent an Optimalist. Instead, we should think of perfectionism and optimalism as lying on a continuum, and each of us tends to a lesser or greater degree to one end or the other of the continuum.

In addition, we may be Optimalists in some areas of our lives and Perfectionists in others. For example, we may be quite forgiving of mistakes we or others make on the job but be thrown into despair when our expectations are not fully met in our relationships. We may have learned to accept that our home is not immaculate, but when it comes to our children, we accept nothing less than perfectly behaved overachievers. In general, the more a Perfectionist cares about something, the more he is likely to approach it with the Perfectionist's particular mind-set. For example, when squash was the center of my life, I experienced intense fear of failure each time I played in a tournament. When I went to college and shifted the focus of my perfectionism to academia, I brought the same paralyzing fear to my studies. By contrast, when I play backgammon, which is a game I enjoy a lot, I do not experience an incapacitating anxiety—or other perfectionist symptoms, for that matter—as it is a less important activity to me (except when I play against my best friend, and chief backgammon rival, Amir).

## Expectation of a Perfect Journey

Perfectionists and Optimalists do not necessarily differ in their aspirations, in the goals they set for themselves. Both can demonstrate the same levels of ambition, the same intense desire to achieve their goals. The difference lies in the ways each approaches the *process* of achieving goals. For the Perfectionist, failure has no role in the journey toward the peak of the mountain; the ideal path toward her goals is the shortest, most direct path—a straight line. Anything that impedes her progress toward the ultimate goal is viewed as an unwelcome obstacle, a hurdle in her path. For the Optimalist, failure is an inevitable part of the journey, of getting from where she is to where she wants to be. She views the optimal journey not as a straight line but as something more like an irregular upward spiral—while the general direction is toward her objective, she knows that there will be numerous deviations along the way.

The Perfectionist likes to think that his path to success can be, and will be, failure free, a straight line. But this does not correspond to reality. Whether we like it or not—and most of us,

**Figure 1.1**

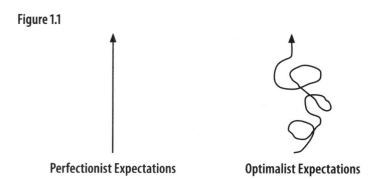

Perfectionist Expectations          Optimalist Expectations

Perfectionists or Optimalists, do not like it—we often stumble, make mistakes, reach dead ends, and need to turn back and start over again. The Perfectionist, with his expectation of a flawless progression along the path to his goals, is unreasonable in his expectations of himself and of his life. He is engaged in wishful thinking and is detached from reality. The Optimalist is grounded in reality: he accepts that the journey will not always be a smooth straight line, that he will inevitably encounter obstacles and detours along the way. He relies on facts and on reason and is in touch with reality.

## Fear of Failure

The central and defining characteristic of perfectionism is the fear of failure. The Perfectionist is driven by this fear; her primary concern is to avoid falling down, deviating, stumbling, erring.[1] She tries in vain to force reality (where some failure is unavoidable) to fit into her straight-line vision of life (where no failure is acceptable)—which is like trying to fit a square peg into a round hole. When faced with the impossibility of this endeavor, she begins to shrink from challenges, to run away from activities where there is some risk of failure. And when she actually fails— when she sooner or later comes face-to-face with her imperfections, with her humanity—she is devastated, which only serves to intensify her fear of failing in the future.

The Optimalist does not like to fail either—nobody does—but she understands that there is no other way to learn and ultimately succeed. In the words of psychologists Shelley Carson and Ellen Langer, the Optimalist understands that "going off course is not always a negative thing, and it can present choices and lessons that may not otherwise have been recognized."[2] To the Optimalist, failure is an opportunity for receiving feedback. Because she isn't intensely afraid of failure, she can learn from it—when she fails at something, she takes her time, "digests" her failure, and learns what set her back. She then tries again, and tries harder. By focusing on growth and improvement, and by rebounding from setbacks, she accepts a more circuitous route to her destination than the Perfectionist who insists on a straight line to her goal. But because the Optimalist neither gives up nor becomes paralyzed by the fear of failure, as the Perfectionist so often does, she has a much better chance of actually reaching her goals.

For the Perfectionist the best possible life—in fact, the *only* life she is prepared to accept—is one devoid of failure. By contrast, the Optimalist knows that the *only* life possible is one in which failure is inevitable, and, given that constraint, the best possible life is one in which she accepts failure and learns from it.

## Focus on the Destination

For the Perfectionist, achieving his goal is the only thing that matters. The process of getting there—the journey—is meaningless to him. He views the journey as simply a series of obstacles that have to be negotiated in order to get to wherever it is that he wants to be. In this sense, the Perfectionist's life is a rat race. He is unable to enjoy the here and now because he is completely engrossed in his obsession with the next promotion, the next prize, the next milestone—which he believes will make him happy. The Perfectionist is aware that he cannot entirely do away with the journey, so he treats it as a bothersome but necessary step in getting to where he wants to be, and he tries to make it as short and as painless as possible.

In the movie *Click*, the hero, Michael Newman, is a consummate Perfectionist. He receives a remote control device that enables him to fast-forward his life. Michael's primary focus is getting promoted at work, which he believes will finally make him happy, so he uses the remote to skip everything he needs to experience on the road to his promotion. He fast-forwards through hard work and hard times but also through all the daily pleasures of life—such as making love to his wife—since they slow down his progress toward his ultimate goal. He considers everything that is not directly related to his end goal an unwelcome detour along the way.

To those around him, Michael seems fully awake, but the effect of using the remote control is that Michael is sedated—not for a few hours to avoid the pain of an operation, but for most of his life—so that he can avoid experiencing the journey, which he perceives as an impediment to his happiness. Michael essentially sleeps through life. Of course, this being a Hollywood movie, Michael realizes the error of his ways and gets a second chance, and this time around he does not make the same mistake: he chooses to experience his life rather than fast-forward through it, and he is a much happier and better person as a result. In real life, Perfectionists who miss everything that matters because they are only focused on their ultimate goal get no second chance.

The Optimist may have the exact same aspirations as the Perfectionist, but he also values the *journey* that takes him to his destination. He understands that along the way there will be detours—some pleasant and desirable, some not. Unlike the Per-

fectionist, he is not so obsessively focused on his goal that the rest
of life ceases to matter. He understands that life is mostly about
what you do on your way to your destination, and he wants to be
fully awake as his own life unfolds.

## The All-or-Nothing Approach

The Perfectionist's universe is ostensibly simple—things are right
or wrong, good or bad, the best or the worst, a success or a failure.
While there is, of course, value in distinguishing between right
and wrong, success and failure—be it in morality or in sports—
the problem with the Perfectionist's approach is that, as far as he
is concerned, these are the *only* categories that exist. There are
no gray areas, no nuances or complexities. As psychologist Asher
Pacht notes, "For Perfectionists, only the extremes of the continuum exist—they are unable to recognize that there is a middle
ground."[3] The Perfectionist takes the existence of extremes to the
extreme.

The all-or-nothing approach manifests itself in different ways.
When playing squash, my resolve was to train exactly like the
world champion, because the only other option I saw was not to
train at all. I was solely focused on the goal of winning and didn't
enjoy playing the game. I experienced an inordinate amount of
pressure when I played in tournaments, especially if I reached the
final, because everything—my total self-worth—hinged on winning a single point, a single game, a single match: either I won the
tournament or I was a total loser. For the person consumed by his
all-or-nothing approach to life, every deviation—no matter how
small or temporary—from the straight line that connects him to
his ultimate objective is experienced as abject failure.

I am not suggesting that the Optimalist is a relativist who
rejects any notion of winning or losing, success or failure, right
or wrong—just because these options signify polar "extremes" on

a continuum.[4] But the Optimalist understands that while these categories do exist—you won the tournament or you lost it, you succeeded to meet your objectives or you failed—there are also countless points between the extremes that may in themselves be necessary and valuable. An Optimalist would have seen what I could not see when I was following Jansher Khan's every move— that there are many other options, many of them healthy and appropriate, between training like the world champion and not training at all. An Optimalist can find value and satisfaction— in other words, happiness—in a less-than-perfect performance, something that I was unable to do as a Perfectionist.

## Defensiveness

Like failure, criticism threatens to expose our flaws. Because of their all-or-nothing approach, Perfectionists perceive every criticism as potentially catastrophic, a dangerous assault on their sense of self-worth. Perfectionists often become extremely antagonistic when criticized and consequently are unable to assess whether there is any merit in the criticism and whether they can learn from it.

Philosopher Mihnea Moldoveanu writes that when "we say we want the truth, what we mean is that we want to be correct"— a perfect description of the Perfectionist. Like most people, the Perfectionist may say that she wants to learn from others. But she is unwilling to pay the price of learning—admitting a shortcoming, flaw, or mistake—because her primary concern is actually to prove that she is right.

Deep down—or, perhaps, not so deep down—the Perfectionist knows that her antagonistic, defensive behavior hurts her and her chances of success, and yet her whole way of understanding herself and the world makes it very difficult for her to change. There are two particular psychological mechanisms that drive her defensiveness: self-enhancement and self-verification.[5] Self-enhancement is the desire to be seen positively by yourself and by others; self-verification is the desire to be perceived accurately by others—to be perceived as you really are (or as you believe you really are). These two mechanisms are often in conflict. For example, a person with low self-esteem may want to look good in the eyes of others (self-enhancement) and at the same time may want to be seen as negatively as she sees herself (self-verification). On the one hand, she wants to be perceived as *worthy*. On the other hand, her low self-esteem makes her feel *unworthy*—and so in order to feel that she is being seen for who she really is, she wants to be seen by others as unworthy. Self-enhancement and self-verification are strong internal drives, and whether one or the other dominates when they are in conflict depends on the individual and the specific situation.

When it comes to perfectionism, self-verification and self-enhancement converge, resulting in excessive defensiveness. The Perfectionist wants to look good (self-enhancement), and therefore she tries to appear flawless by deflecting criticism. The picture that the Perfectionist has of herself—the only picture she tolerates—is of flawlessness, and she goes to great lengths to convince others that the way she views herself is indeed correct (self-verification). She will defend her ego and her self-perception at all costs and will not allow criticism that could expose her as less than perfect.

The Optimalist, by contrast, is open to suggestions. She recognizes the value of feedback—whether it takes the form of failure or success when she attempts something or of praise or criticism from others. Though she may not like it when her flaws are pointed out—most people do not enjoy being criticized, just as most people do not like to fail—she nevertheless takes the time to openly and honestly assess whether the criticism is valid and then asks herself how she can learn and improve from it. Recognizing the value of feedback, she actively seeks it and is grateful to those who are willing to point out her shortcomings and her virtues.

## Faultfinding

"The fault-finder," Henry David Thoreau said, "will find faults even in paradise."[6] The Perfectionist's obsession with failure focuses his attention on the empty part of the glass. No matter how successful he is, his shortcomings and imperfections eclipse all his accomplishments. Because the Perfectionist engages in both faultfinding and all-or-nothing thinking, he tends to see the glass as totally empty—the faultfinding approach finds some emptiness, whereas the all-or-nothing approach takes it to the extreme of total emptiness. Because he is under the illusion that a straight-line journey is possible and that failure can be entirely avoided, he is constantly on the lookout for imperfections and deviations from the ideal path. Seeking faults, he finds them, of course—even in paradise.

Ralph Waldo Emerson wrote, "To different minds, the same world is a hell, and a heaven."[7] Our subjective interpretation of the world matters; what we focus on makes a difference. A less-than-stellar athletic or academic performance, for instance, will be perceived by the Perfectionist as a catastrophe and might lead him to avoid all further challenges. The Optimalist, by contrast, although he will be disappointed by his failures, is more likely to consider them as learning opportunities; failures, rather than paralyze him, may in fact stimulate extra effort. Optimalists tend to be *benefit finders*—the sort of people who find the silver lining in the dark cloud, who make lemonade out of lemons, who look on the bright side of life, and who do not fault writers for using too many clichés. With a knack for turning setbacks into opportunities, the Optimalist goes through life with an overall sense of optimism.

However, while the Optimalist tends to focus on the potential benefits inherent in any situation, he also acknowledges that not every negative event has a positive aspect, that there are many wrongs in the world, and that at times a negative reaction to events is very appropriate. A person who can never see the negative is a detached Pollyanna, and just as unrealistic as the person who sees only the negative.

## Harshness

The Perfectionist can be extremely hard on herself, as well as on others. When she makes mistakes, when she fails, she is unforgiving. Her harshness stems from her belief that it is actually possible (and, of course, desirable) to go through life smoothly, without blunders. Errors are avoidable—they are in *her* power to avoid—and therefore, she regards being harsh on herself as a form of taking responsibility. The Perfectionist takes the notion of taking responsibility to its unhealthy extreme.

The Optimalist, for her part, takes responsibility for her mistakes and learns from her failures, but she also accepts that making mistakes and experiencing failure are unavoidable. Therefore, the Optimalist is a great deal more understanding when it comes to her failures; she is much more forgiving of herself.

The Perfectionist's harshness and the Optimalist's tendency to forgive mistakes extend to the way they treat others. Our behavior toward others is often a reflection of our treatment of ourselves. Being kind and compassionate toward oneself usually translates to kind and compassionate behavior toward others; the converse is also the case, as harshness toward the self often translates to harshness toward others.

## Rigidity

For the Perfectionist there is only one way to get where he wants to go, and that route is a straight line. The path he sets for himself (as well as for others) is rigid and static, and the language he tends to use to communicate his intentions is categorical, even moralistic: *ought, have to, must, should.*

Feelings are irrelevant to his decision-making process. He views them as harmful, because they may change, often in unpredictable ways, and they do not conform to his *"musts"* and *"have tos."* Surprise is dangerous; the future ought to be known. Change is the enemy; spontaneity and improvisation are too risky. Playfulness is unacceptable, especially in those areas that he cares about most, unless the parameters are clear and well defined in advance.

Rigidity in the Perfectionist stems, at least in part, from his obsessive need for control. The Perfectionist tries to control every aspect of his life because he fears that if he were to relinquish some control, his world would fall apart. If he needs to get something done at work or elsewhere, he prefers to do it himself. He does not trust other people, unless he is certain that they will follow his instructions to the letter. His fear of letting go is closely associated with his fear of failure.

Rigidity manifests itself in another way as well. Imagine a person who, committed to his goal of becoming a partner in a consulting firm, spends seventy hours a week in the office. He is unhappy at work and knows that the job at which he felt most fulfilled was when he worked at a restaurant during his summers in college. But he refuses to change his planned course of action— perhaps he even refuses to admit to himself that he is miserable— and continues along the same path toward partnership; regardless of the cost, he refuses to give up on his goal, refuses to "fail" at becoming a partner.

The Optimalist also sets ambitious goals for himself, but, unlike the Perfectionist, he is not chained to these commitments. He might decide, for example, to continue investing time and effort in his goal of becoming a partner at the firm but at the same time relax his schedule slightly, or take some time off, in order to explore whether opening a restaurant might be the right thing for him after all.

In other words, the Optimalist does not chart his direction according to a rigid map but rather based on a more fluid compass. The compass gives him the confidence to meander, to take the circuitous path. While he has a clear sense of direction, he is also dynamic and adaptable, open to different alternatives, able to cope with surprises and unpredictable twists and turns. Accepting that different paths may lead to his destination, he is flexible, not spineless, open to possibilities without being purposeless.

| The Perfectionist | The Optimalist |
| --- | --- |
| Journey as a straight line | Journey as an irregular spiral |
| Fear of failure | Failure as feedback |
| Focus on destination | Focus on journey and destination |
| All-or-nothing thinking | Nuanced, complex thinking |
| Defensive | Open to suggestions |
| Faultfinder | Benefit finder |
| Harsh | Forgiving |
| Rigid, static | Adaptable, dynamic |

**TIME-IN** Can you relate to some of the characteristics associated with perfectionism? How do these characteristics affect your life?

## Consequences

Of course, most Perfectionists do not exhibit all of the perfectionist qualities that I have discussed so far. Nor do they exhibit their perfectionist qualities to the same degree in every situation. But the more they exhibit these qualities, the higher their susceptibility to a whole range of disorders, problems, and challenges associated with perfectionism. These include low self-esteem, eating disorders, sexual dysfunction, depression, anxiety, obsessive-compulsive disorder, psychosomatic disorders, chronic fatigue syndrome, alcoholism, social phobia, panic disorder, a paralyzing tendency to procrastination, and serious difficulties in relationships.[8] I will elaborate on a few of these consequences.

## Low Self-Esteem

Perfectionism has a devastating impact on self-esteem. Think of a child growing up in a home where, regardless of what he does, he is constantly criticized and put down. Imagine an employee whose shortcomings are constantly highlighted by her boss. Could such a child or an employee enjoy healthy self-esteem? Unlikely. On the contrary, it is likely that, to the extent that they gained any self-esteem elsewhere, it will be squeezed out of them in no time in such an environment. None of us would want to be that child or that employee and live or work under such conditions. Yet the Perfectionist not only lives in precisely this kind of environment; he imposes it upon himself.

Because the life of a Perfectionist is an endless rat race, his enjoyment of success is short lived. He is far more likely to dwell on his failures than on his successes, because when he succeeds in achieving a goal, he immediately starts worrying about the next goal and what would happen if he fails to reach it. The all-or-nothing mind-set leads Perfectionists to transform every setback they encounter into a catastrophe, an assault on their very worth as human beings. Their sense of self inevitably suffers as their faultfinding turns inward.

Today, as I look back on my career as a squash player, I am proud of my efforts, of my dedication to my goal, and of what I accomplished. At the time, though, my self-esteem took a constant beating, as a result of failure or the imminent threat of failure. Very few people then were aware that I suffered from low self-esteem—it was unthinkable to the Perfectionist in me to expose any weakness or imperfection. The Perfectionist constantly engages in self-enhancement, and to the outside world he tries to communicate the flawless facade of what Nathaniel Branden calls pseudo self-esteem: "the pretense at self-confidence and self-respect we do not actually feel."[9]

Unlike the Perfectionist, the Optimalist does not reside in a psychological prison of his own making. In fact, over time, the self-esteem of the Optimalist increases. One of the wishes that I always have for my students is that they should fail more often (although they are understandably not thrilled to hear me tell them so). If they fail frequently, it means that they try frequently, that they put themselves on the line and challenge themselves. It is only from the experience of challenging ourselves that we learn and grow, and we often develop and mature much more from our failures than from our successes. Moreover, when we put ourselves on the line, when we fall down and get up again, we become stronger and more resilient.

In their work on self-esteem, Richard Bednar and Scott Peterson point out that the very experience of coping—dealing with challenges and risking failure—increases our self-confidence.[10] If we avoid hardships and challenges because we may fail, the message we are sending ourselves is that we are unable to deal with difficulty—in this case, unable to handle failure—and our self-esteem suffers as a result. But if we do challenge ourselves, the message we internalize is that we are resilient enough to handle potential failure. Taking on challenges instead of avoiding them has a greater long-term effect on our self-esteem than winning or losing, failing or succeeding.

Paradoxically, our overall self-confidence and our belief in our own ability to deal with setbacks may be reinforced when we fail, because we realize that the beast we had always feared—failure—is not as terrifying as we thought it was. Like the Wizard of Oz, who turns out to be much less frightening when he is exposed, so failure turns out to be far less threatening when confronted directly. Over the years, by avoiding failure, the Perfectionist invests it with much more power than it deserves. The pain associated with the fear of failure is usually more intense than the pain following an actual failure.

In her 2008 commencement speech at Harvard, J. K. Rowling, author of the Harry Potter books, talked about the value of failure:

> Failure meant a stripping away of the inessential. . . . I was set free, because my greatest fear had already been realized, and I was still alive, and I still had a daughter whom I adored, and I had an old typewriter and a big idea. And so rock bottom became the solid foundation on which I rebuilt my life. . . . Failure gave me an inner security that I had never attained by passing examinations. Failure taught me things about myself that I could have learned no other way. I discovered that I had a strong will, and more discipline than I had suspected; I also found out that I had friends whose value was truly above rubies. . . . The knowledge that you have emerged wiser and stronger from setbacks means that you are, ever after, secure in your ability to survive. You will never truly know yourself, or the strength of your relationships, until both have been tested by adversity.

We can only learn to deal with failure by actually experiencing failure, by living through it. The earlier we face difficulties and drawbacks, the better prepared we are to deal with the inevitable obstacles along our path.

Talent and success without the moderating effect of failure can be detrimental, even dangerous. Until Vincent Foster was appointed President Bill Clinton's deputy White House counsel, his career ascent had been remarkably smooth. According to one of his colleagues, Foster had experienced no professional setbacks, "Never. Not even a tiny one . . . he seemed to glide through life." Then the Clinton administration and Foster's office came under scrutiny, and he "felt he had failed to protect the President by keeping the process under control." This perceived failure devastated him, and, unable to deal with anything short of total success, he committed suicide. Nothing in his prior experience had prepared him to deal with the psychological impact of failure.[11]

This is not to say that failure at any point in life is pleasant or easy (it is neither) or even that there is no such thing as devastating failure. However, not trying so that we can avoid failure turns out to be a lot more damaging to our long-term success and overall well-being than putting ourselves on the line and failing. As the Danish theologian Søren Kierkegaard noted, "To dare is to lose one's footing momentarily. Not to dare, is to lose oneself." When we dare, when we cope, we are much more likely to fail—and there is certainly a price tag on that. But the price of not daring and not failing is a great deal higher.

**TIME-IN** Think of a challenge that you took on, something that you dared to do. What did you learn, and in what ways did you grow from the experience?

## Eating Disorders

In a review article on the link between eating disorders and perfectionism, psychologist Anna Bardone-Cone and her colleagues cite research suggesting that "the aspect of perfectionism associated with the tendency to interpret mistakes as failures is most strongly associated with eating disorders."[12] Perfectionists are susceptible to eating disorders because in their all-or-nothing mindset only extreme failure or extreme success exist—and therefore, if they are concerned about their body image, the choice that they see for themselves is between being fat or being skinny, binging or starving. There is no healthy middle ground.

The media feeds these perfectionist attitudes. The perfect way to look—the "all" as opposed to the "nothing"—is not left for men's or women's imagination but rather shoved in our faces on magazine covers and billboards. The Perfectionist then overlooks the fact that most people do not look like supermodels—and that even supermodels do not look like supermodels. Editing software brushes away natural wrinkles or lines, leaving behind suffering humans in its digital dust.

Being flesh and blood rather than perfected digital images, the Perfectionists always find some fault in their appearance. Their all-or-nothing mind-set magnifies every blemish, every deviation from their idealized image. They become obsessed with the extra two pounds they may have gained or with the wrinkle that they think mars their complexion. Perfectionists then take extreme measures to eliminate these perceived imperfections, whether through repeated plastic surgery, invasive beauty treatments, or starvation.

When Perfectionists attempt to lose weight, they usually adopt an extreme dietary regime, which they then follow to the letter. But when eventually, for whatever reason, they are tempted to take a bite of a forbidden food, their sense of having failed is overwhelming, and they punish themselves both psychologically and physically. Often, they will end up devouring the entire gallon of ice cream they tasted and then gorge on everything else in sight. In their all-or-nothing world, they are either on a perfect regime of dieting or off the diet completely. The irony is that even in the midst of eating the gallon of ice cream, Perfectionists derive little, if any, enjoyment from it; the knowledge that they have failed prevents them from enjoying what they are eating.

Optimalists are not necessarily oblivious to the way they look or to what they eat. However, the standards they hold themselves to are human rather than superhuman. They understand the difference between a multidimensional real person and a two-dimensional picture that has been worked on pixel by pixel. And if they are concerned with following a healthy diet or with their weight, they do not berate themselves if they succumb to temptation once in a while. Slipping up from time to time will not drive them from one behavioral extreme to another: they recognize and accept their own humanity—in other words, their fallibility—and they are compassionate toward themselves. At times, they follow Oscar Wilde's advice and get rid of temptation by yielding to it—enjoying a delicious scoop of ice cream.

## Sexual Dysfunction

Perfectionism is one of the leading psychological causes of sexual dysfunction in both men and women. A man's expectation of flawless sexual performance may lead to erectile dysfunction. For a woman, the need to perform may be so distracting that she fails to become aroused and enjoy sex. For both sexes, each sexual encounter becomes a test, with potential far-reaching ramifications. The evening is either going to be a mind-blowing love-making session or a total disaster. The all-or-nothing mind-set catastrophizes a single imperfect performance and, through the process of a self-fulfilling prophecy, can lead to impotence in the man and sexual arousal disorder in the woman.

Being overcritical—of one's own body, of one's sexual performance, of one's partner—can lead to diminished enjoyment of sex. Moreover, the focus of the Perfectionist on the destination at the expense of the journey leads to an obsession with orgasms and may actually diminish the pleasure of lovemaking.

Optimalists accept the imperfections of their bodies and their sexual performance as natural and human, and therefore, they are able to enjoy sex. Because they are not focused on the faults they or their partners might discover or uncover, they are free to experience the pleasures of mind and body in love.

## Depression

Perfectionists are at risk for depression. This is not surprising when you consider that among the causes of depression are faultfinding, an all-or-nothing mentality, and a focus on the goal to the exclusion of any enjoyment of the journey. We spend most of our life engaged in the journey, because the actual moments when we reach our destinations and achieve our goals are necessarily fleeting. If most of what we derive from the journey is unhappiness and pain, then our life as a whole is unhappy and painful.

As we have seen, Perfectionists have a tendency to low self-esteem because their faultfinding is directed inward, something which can also lead to depression. Depression, however, is also caused when the Perfectionist's tendency to find fault is directed *outward*. The potential for happiness is inside us and all around us; unfortunately, so is the potential for unhappiness. And because the Perfectionist finds fault with everything, the actual circumstances of her life matter very little, because she will manage to find something wrong, magnify it out of all proportion, and thus ruin any possibility of enjoying what she has or what she does.

The Optimalist experiences sadness at times, of course, but she takes each difficult experience in stride. She is able to take a "this too shall pass" approach to problems, and, with her focus on the experience of the journey, she spends much of her time in a positive state. Her life is not without its ups and downs. She has moments of deep sadness and frustration too. But her life is not marred by the constant fear of failure or the magnified impact of actual failure.

The Optimalist is also better equipped to handle challenges. Psychologist Carl Rogers identifies the essential progress in therapy as one in which the client realizes that she is "a fluid process, not a fixed and static entity; a flowing river of change, not a block of solid material; a continually changing constellation of potentialities, not a fixed quantity of traits."[13] Rogers is, in essence, describing the Optimalist whose flexibility allows her to learn rather than stagnate, to grow stronger rather than grow weaker, to navigate through treacherous waters rather than sink into emotional disorder.

## Anxiety Disorders

Perfectionism not only causes anxiety disorders but can itself be understood as a form of anxiety disorder—*failure anxiety*. Since the all-or-nothing approach does not distinguish minor failures from major ones, virtually every situation has within it the potential for catastrophe, and this is something that the Perfectionist is always aware of. As a result of obsessively worrying about these "catastrophes" that are just around the corner, the Perfectionist experiences ongoing anxiety and at times panic.

There is another element, though, that accounts for both anxiety and depression among Perfectionists, and that is their rigid, inflexible mind-set. One of the reasons why depression and anxiety are on the rise throughout the world stems from the fast rate of change—markets change daily, technology advances by the nanosecond, and new ways of doing and being are constantly advertised and promoted. The Perfectionist's fixed and inflexible perception of the right way of doing things, the right way to live, is constantly challenged by the outside world—a world that is fluid and, at times, unpredictable.

Perfectionism was a problem three thousand years ago, but given the relatively static world it was possible to survive and even thrive being a Perfectionist. Today—and increasingly more so by the day—shifting from perfectionism toward optimalism is becoming vital. A rigid mind-set is ill-suited for modern fluidity—which is one of the reasons why levels of depression, anxiety, and suicide rates among the young are rising, in the United States, in China—which is experiencing unprecedented growth—and throughout our flat world.

The Optimalist, being more flexible and open to deviations, is better able to cope with the ever-changing environment. While at times he, too, struggles with change, he has the willingness and the self-confidence necessary to deal with the unpredictable and the uncertain. Change is not a threat but a challenge; the unknown is not frightening but fascinating.

**TIME-IN** Are you struggling with any of the issues associated with perfectionism? Where in your life are you an Optimalist?

## Success

Many Perfectionists understand that their perfectionism harms them, but they are reluctant to change because they believe that while perfectionism may not make you happy, it does make you successful. Echoing John Stuart Mill's choice between being an unhappy Socrates and a happy fool, the Perfectionist believes his choice is either to be an unsuccessful (and perhaps happy) slacker and a successful (albeit unhappy) Perfectionist. Not wanting to be a slacker, he chooses the other extreme, placated by his belief in the philosophy of "No pain, no gain." The Optimalist, however, challenges the Perfectionist's philosophical rhyme with his own, as he does it "Better with pleasure" (sorry!).

And, indeed, research indicates that while there are, of course, highly successful Perfectionists, all other things being equal, an Optimalist is more likely to be successful. There are a number of reasons why, including the following.

## Learning from Failure

To remain employable, let alone competitive, we must constantly learn and grow, and to learn and grow, we must fail. It is no coincidence that the most successful people throughout history are also the ones who have failed the most. Thomas Edison, who registered 1,093 patents—including ones associated with the lightbulb, the phonograph, the telegraph, and cement—proudly declared that he failed his way to success. When someone pointed out to him that he had failed ten thousand times while working on one of his inventions, Edison responded, "I have not failed. I've just found ten thousand ways that won't work."

Babe Ruth, considered by many the greatest baseball player in history, hit 714 career home runs—a record that held for thirty-nine years. But he also topped the league five times in the number of strikeouts.

Michael Jordan, arguably the greatest sportsman of our time, reminds his admirers that even he is human: "I've missed more than nine thousand shots in my career. I've lost almost three hundred games. Twenty-six times, I've been trusted to take the game-winning shot and missed. I've failed over and over and over again in my life. And that is why I succeed."

And then there is the man who at the age of twenty-two lost his job. A year later he tried his luck in politics, ran for the state legislature, and was defeated. He next tried his hand at business again and failed. At the age of twenty-seven he had a nervous breakdown. But he bounced back, and at the age of thirty-four, having gained some experience, he ran for Congress. He lost. Five years later, the same thing happened again. Clearly not discouraged by failure, he set his goals even higher and ran for the Senate at the age of forty-six. When that failed, he sought nomination for vice president, again unsuccessfully. Just shy of his fiftieth birthday, after decades of professional failures and defeats, he ran again for the Senate and was defeated. But two years later this man, Abraham Lincoln, became the president of the United States.

These are stories of exceptional people, but the pattern of their stories is common to millions of others who have achieved small or great feats by failing their way to success. Failure is essential in achieving success—though it is of course not sufficient for achieving success. In other words, while failure does not guarantee success, the absence of failure will almost always guarantee the absence of success. Those who understand that failure is inextricably linked with achievement are the ones who learn, grow, and ultimately do well. *Learn to fail, or fail to learn.*

The comfortable relationship that Optimalists have with failure makes them more willing to experiment and to take risks and makes them more open to feedback. In a study that hit close to home for me, Perfectionists were shown to be weaker writers than non-Perfectionists because "they took pains to avoid allowing other people to view samples of their writing, thereby insulating themselves from feedback that could have improved writing skills."[14] A genuine desire to learn—whether from the feedback of other people or from the feedback that failure itself can provide—is a prerequisite for success, whether one is in banking, teaching, athletics, engineering, or any other profession.

## Peak Performance

Psychologists Robert Yerkes and J. D. Dodson show that performance improves as levels of mental and physiological arousal increase—until a point when further increase in arousal leads to poorer performance.[15] In other words, when levels of arousal are too low (lethargy or complacency) and when levels of arousal are too high (anxiety or fear), performance is likely to suffer. So when are people most likely to perform at their best? When they experience excitement, the midpoint between feeling lethargic and feeling anxious.

Top performers in sports, business, science, politics, and every other area of human achievement are usually very disappointed

**Figure 1.2**

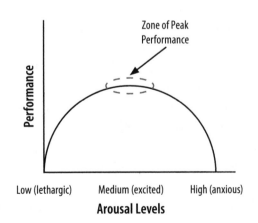

when their efforts fall short of their high expectations. However, they are not paralyzed by an intense fear of possible failure, and when they do fail (as we all do, from time to time), they do not catastrophize their failures. The combination of on the one hand striving for success and on the other accepting failure as a natural part of life enables them to experience the kind of excitement that leads to peak performance.

## Enjoying the Journey

Howard Gardner, among the leading thinkers in the area of education, studied the lives of extraordinary people such as Gandhi, Freud, Picasso, and Einstein, as well as of other accomplished though lesser-known individuals.[16] Gardner found that it takes approximately ten years of intense work to acquire the level of expertise required to thrive in any field—from business to athletics, from medicine to art. And of course the hard work is not over after ten years—just as much effort, and sometimes even more effort, is necessary to sustain success.

For the Perfectionist, sustaining this sort of effort can be extremely difficult. The Perfectionist's obsession with the destination and her inability to enjoy the journey eventually saps her desire and motivation, so that she is less likely to put in the hard work necessary for success. No matter how motivated she may be at the beginning, the strain of sustaining an effort for long periods of time eventually becomes intolerable if the entire process—the journey—is unhappy. There comes a point when, despite the Perfectionist's motivation to succeed, part of her will begin to want to give up, just in order to avoid further pain. No matter how intensely she may want the promotion from middle to senior management, the Perfectionist may find that because the journey is so long—and it always lasts much, much longer than that brief moment when the destination is reached—she cannot bear to sustain it. As a result, she may begin to spend as little time as possible at work and expends as little energy as she can get away with in the accomplishment of her daily tasks.

The Optimalist is able to enjoy the journey while remaining focused on her destination. While she may not necessarily experience a smooth, easy ride to success—she struggles, she falls, she has her doubts, and she experiences pain at times—her overall journey is far more pleasant than the Perfectionist's. She is motivated by the pull of the destination (the goal she wants to achieve) as well as by the pull of the journey (the day to day that she enjoys). She feels both a sense of daily joy and lasting fulfillment.

There is another way in which focusing only on the destination harms the Perfectionist. Much research illustrates that perfectionism leads to procrastination and paralysis.[17] The Perfectionist puts off certain work temporarily (procrastination) or permanently (paralysis) both because work for her is painful and because inaction provides an excuse for failure. If I don't try, she thinks to herself, I won't fail. In the perverse logic of the Perfectionist, where only outcomes matter, avoiding failure by avoiding work itself makes a certain kind of sense. By trying to preclude the possibility of failure, however, the Perfectionist is of course also precluding the possibility of success.

## Using Time Efficiently

The all-or-nothing approach—the idea that work that is not done perfectly is not worth doing at all—leads to procrastination and, more generally, to inefficient use of time. To do something perfectly (assuming perfection is even possible) often requires extraordinary effort that may not be justified in the context of the task at hand. Given that time is a precious resource, perfectionism comes at a high price.

Where appropriate, the Optimalist will devote to a particular task as much time as the Perfectionist would. But not all jobs are equally important, and not all require equal attention. For instance, making sure that every O-ring is sealed before launching a spacecraft is clearly critical, and nothing short of perfect work should be tolerated. However, it may be less appropriate for an engineer working at the space station to fuss for a long while over the colors of a chart on an internal memo about departmental budgets.

During my first two years in college, I devoted tremendous amounts of time to every assignment in every course, and I studied equally hard for every exam. Over time, as I recognized the heavy toll that perfectionism was taking, I shifted toward the optimalist end of the continuum. My approach changed, and I adopted the 80/20 rule, also known as the Pareto Principle.

## The 80/20 Rule

This principle is named after Italian economist Vilfredo Pareto, who observed the 80/20 phenomenon—that, in general, 20 percent of the population of a country owns 80 percent of the country's wealth, that 20 percent of a company's clients generate 80 percent of its revenues, and so on. More recently, the principle has been applied to time management by Richard Koch and Marc Mancini, who suggest that we can make better use of our time by investing our efforts in the 20 percent that will get us 80 percent of the results we want to achieve.[18] For example, it may take between two and three hours to write that perfect report, but in thirty minutes we may be able to produce a report that is sufficiently good for our purpose.

In college, once I stopped being a Perfectionist who needed to read every word in every book that my professors assigned, I began to apply the Pareto Principle, skimming most of the assigned readings but then identifying and focusing on the 20 percent of the text that would yield the most "bang for the buck." I still wanted to do well academically. That much hadn't changed. What did change was my "A or nothing" approach, which had guided me as a Perfectionist. While my grade point average did initially suffer slightly, I was able to devote more time to important extracurricular activities, such as playing squash, developing my career as a public speaker, and, last but not least, spending time with my friends. I ended up not only a great deal happier than I had been during my first two years in college but also, looking at that period in my life as a whole (as opposed to through the narrow lens of my grade point average), more successful. The 80/20 rule has continued to serve me well in my career.

**TIME-IN** Think about your 80/20 allocation of time. Where can you do less? Where do you want to invest more?

Perfectionism manifests itself in different ways and to differing degrees in each person. Consequently, some of the characteristics that I have discussed in this chapter may be relevant to some people and not to others. The first step, therefore, is to be open rather than defensive and to identify those characteristics that are relevant to you. The second step is to better understand these characteristics and their consequences. Finally, the last step is to bring about the sought-after change through a combination of action and reflection—by thinking about the Time-Ins and working through the exercises in this book.

Moving toward the optimalist side of the continuum is a lifelong project, one that only ends when life itself ends. It is a journey that demands much patience, time, and effort—and a journey that can be delightfully pleasant and infinitely rewarding.

# EXERCISES

## Taking Action

Research by psychologist Daryl Bem shows that we form attitudes about ourselves in the same way that we form attitudes about others, namely, through observation.[19] If we see a man helping others, we conclude that he is kind; if we see a woman standing up for her beliefs, we conclude that she is principled and courageous. Similarly, we draw conclusions about ourselves by observing our own behavior. When we act kindly or courageously, our attitudes are likely to shift in the direction of our action, and we tend to feel, and see ourselves as, kinder and more courageous. Through this mechanism, which Bem calls Self-Perception Theory, behaviors can change attitudes over time. And because perfectionism is an attitude, we can begin to change it through our behavior. In other words, by observing ourselves behave as Optimalists do—taking risks, venturing outside our comfort zone, being open rather than defensive, falling down and getting up again—we become Optimalists.

For this exercise, think of something that you would like to do but have always been reluctant to try for fear of failing. Then go ahead and do it! Audition for a part in a play, try out for a sports team, ask someone out on a date, start writing that book that you've always wanted to write. As you pursue the activity, and elsewhere in your life, behave in ways that an Optimalist would, even if initially you have to fake it. Look for additional opportunities to venture outside your comfort zone, ask for feedback and help, admit your mistakes, and so on.

Have fun with this exercise. Don't worry if you fail and have to try again. In writing, reflect on how this process of learning from failure applies to other areas of your life.

## Keeping a Journal About Failure

In their work on mindfulness and self-acceptance, psychologists Shelley Carson and Ellen Langer note that "when people allow themselves to investigate their mistakes and see what mistakes have to teach them, they think mindfully about themselves and their world, and they increase their ability not only to accept themselves and their mistakes but to be grateful for their mistakes as directions for future growth."[20] The following exercise is about investigating your mistakes.

Take fifteen minutes of your time and write about an event or a situation in which you failed.[21] Describe what you did, the thoughts that went through your mind, how you felt about it then, and how you feel about it now as you are writing. Has the passage of time changed your perspective on the event? What are the lessons that you have learned from the experience? Can you think of other benefits that came about as a result of the failure, that made the experience a valuable one?

Repeat this exercise two or three additional times, either on consecutive days or over a period of a few weeks. You can write about the same failure each time, or about a different one.

# 2

# Accepting Emotions

---

**Those who don't know how to weep with their whole heart don't know how to laugh either.**

—*Golda Meir*

Yom Kippur, 1973. My first memory.

The phone rings in our apartment in Ramat Gan, Israel. My dad picks up. He whispers to my mom. They look at each other, and then at me. I look into their pale faces. My dad walks to his room. I run after him. He puts on his army uniform. He ties the laces of his boots. He gets up. He runs his hand through my hair. I follow him outside to our turquoise Ford Cortina. My friend Esti is standing next to her father. He too is in uniform. All the fathers are in uniform standing by their cars. I know the names of all the cars in our neighborhood.

"Daddy, you are not allowed to drive on Yom Kippur."

"Sweetie, there's a war on," he says, blackening the lights of our car with shoe polish.

"Why are you painting the lights?" I ask.

"So the airplanes don't see us in the dark," he responds.

"The Phantoms?"

"No, the MIGs."

I plead, "But we have to go back to temple. The shofar."

"You'll go with Mommy," he says, and his lips gently touch my cheek. He gets into the car, turns on the ignition, and drives off.

I want to run after him, but my mom holds me tight, and I cry, and I cry, and I cannot stop crying. Shaul, our elderly next-door neighbor, says to me, "Do you want to be a soldier when you grow up, like Daddy?"

"Yes," I manage, between sobs.

"Soldiers don't cry."

I stop crying.

The old port of Jaffa, 1989. A few feet away from me, a fisherman and his wife sit close together, gazing at a distant ship and now and then at each other. I am gazing at my girlfriend, whom I have not seen for two weeks, which felt like an eternity. The full moon casts its light on her delicate face, and watching her I feel my tears welling up. I look away. She draws closer. Her fingers pass through my hair. I want to tell her how much I love her. I don't.

Herzliya Squash Club, 1991. The finals of the Israeli nationals. I am the favorite to win the championship for a record fourth time. I lose. The trophy ceremony is excruciating, but I am stoic. I say and do all the right things, until it finally ends and my girlfriend and I leave. As soon as we do, she bursts into tears.

"Why are you crying?" I ask her.

"I'm crying because you're not."

The next day she brings me a recording of a song whose lyrics include the phrase, "Give me the strength to be weak." I allow the tears to well up.

Experiences in my early childhood taught me to suppress my emotions, to hide my pain. It took me years to unlearn this harmful habit and give myself the permission to feel, the permission to be human. My most significant psychological breakthrough came when I realized—truly *internalized* the notion—that it was all right for me to be sad, that there was nothing wrong with feeling dispirited, scared, lonely, or anxious. That simple realization, that it was OK to *feel*, was the first step of a long journey, one that is ongoing, with its fair share of progress and setbacks, victories and failures.

In the previous chapter I focused on the Perfectionist's rejection of failure in the context of performance. In this chapter I will focus on the rejection of failure in the context of emotions—on what the Perfectionist perceives as emotional failure.

We've seen that the Perfectionist has a very rigid view of what her life (and the lives of others, for that matter) should be like, and how she rejects as unacceptable any deviation from that ideal. In the realm of performance, of personal or professional success, the Perfectionist's ideal is a straight-line journey to success. In the realm of emotions, the Perfectionist's ideal is in most cases a life that comprises an unbroken chain of positive feelings. I say in most cases, because some Perfectionists perceive the tormented life as the ideal: the tortured soul, the suffering artist, the beleaguered outcast, the wronged victim, and so on. For them, the ideal that they yearn for, whether consciously or unconsciously, is a life that comprises an unbroken chain of painful emotions, and they reject any positive emotions they may feel. However, regardless of whether the Perfectionist's ideal is of an unbroken chain of positive emotions or negative ones, she rejects all deviations from the emotional state that she has claimed as her own. Our nature, and the reality of living, is such that whether we like it or not, we experience the full range of emotion. And if we do not give ourselves the permission to experience it, the inevitable result is intense painful emotions or, perhaps even worse, the failure to feel any emotion at all.

In contrast, the Optimalist sees life as it is: fluid, changing, dynamic. Just as she accepts failure as part and parcel of the human experience, she accepts painful (and pleasurable) emotions as an inevitable consequence of being alive. She is open to what the world offers and is able to accept life and the variety of experiences and emotions that it has to offer. She is therefore more likely than the Perfectionist to actually experience and express her emotions—by crying when she needs to, by sharing her feelings with her friends, or by writing about her feelings in her journal.

The emotional life that the Perfectionist expects is one of a constant high; the Optimalist expects his life to include emotional ups, emotional downs, and everything in between. The Perfectionist rejects painful emotions that do not meet his expectation of an unwavering flow of positive emotions; the Optimalist permits himself to experience the full range of human emotions.

Many people learn early on, as I did, to hide and suppress their feelings, the pleasurable as well as the painful ones. We may have been told that boys don't cry, that expressing pleasure at our accomplishments was evidence of unbecoming pride, or that

**Figure 2.1**

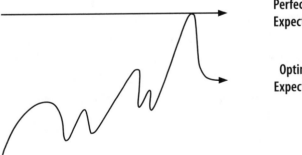

Perfectionist
Expectations

Optimalist
Expectations

wanting something that someone else had was greedy. We may have been taught that being attracted to someone and yearning to express that physically was dirty and shameful or, conversely, that feeling shy and nervous about opening ourselves up emotionally and physically was uncool and shameful. Unlearning the lessons of childhood and early adulthood is hard, which is why it is difficult for so many of us to open ourselves to the flow of emotions.

TIME-IN Can you recall early experiences that taught you to express or suppress emotions?

## Let Your Feelings Flow

Imagine Main Street if we didn't rein in our emotions. Rude comments tossed at a passerby who fails to meet our unrefined aesthetic sensibilities; obscenities running wild each time our expectations are frustrated; an unrestricted flow of tears, of joy or misery, in response to memories that are evoked no matter where we are; an uninvited growl and then a leap at a sexual object walking past. The rules of the jungle—the product of impulse, impatience, and untamed power—would launch a hostile takeover of our concrete jungles. Fortunately, we learn to suppress our base instincts, to civilize our uncivilized urges—to hide our raw feelings and tame the ignoble savage.

Social ties would not hold—communities, families, and relationships would fall apart—if our emotions were always exposed. We have all at some time felt a primal emotion—be it envy, anger, desire—toward a friend or colleague, which, if revealed, would have endangered our relationship with that person. We have all in our imagination violated some of the commandments that hold society together—lusted after our neighbor's partner, felt angry enough to hurt someone. We learn early on to control our emotions in public—a necessity in order to survive, let alone thrive, in the world. But as with most human interventions in nature, there are also side effects to suppressing our true feelings.

While it's at times necessary to keep certain emotions out of sight (when we are with others), it may be harmful to try to keep them out of mind (when we are alone). We are taught that it is improper to display our anxiety or to cry in public, so we hold our emotions back in private as well. Anger does not win us friends, and over time we lose our ability to express and experience anger altogether. We extinguish our anxiety, fear, and rage for the sake of being pleasant and easy to get along with—and in the process of getting others to accept us, we reject ourselves. Denying ourselves the permission to acknowledge and truly experience "undesirable" emotions is detrimental to our well-being and an obstacle to becoming an Optimalist.

## The Cost of Suppressing Emotions

Much has been written about the cost to our psychological well-being of suppressing our emotions. Psychologists such as Carl Rogers and Nathaniel Branden have illustrated how we damage our self-esteem when we deny our feelings. Richard Wenzlaff and Daniel Wegner, in their research on thought suppression, demonstrate that "the tendency to avoid thinking about traumatic or anxiety-producing topics may prompt the return of those topics to mind, and so activate a cycle that could perpetuate anxiety disorders." In other research it was found that "higher levels of self-reported suppression of depressive thoughts were associated with a worsening of depressive symptoms." Rather than trying to suppress or avoid certain thoughts, Wenzlaff and Wegner suggest that a more helpful approach for dealing with anxiety and depression would be "accepting and expressing unwanted thoughts."[1]

When the Perfectionist rejects his emotions, not only by refusing to express them but also by refusing to allow himself to experience them, these emotions intensify—which is the opposite of what he intended. Try the following simple experiment, suggested by psychologist Daniel Wegner. For the next ten seconds, keep telling yourself not to think of a white bear. Do not, under any circumstances, think of a white bear. . . .

In all likelihood, you could not *stop* thinking about a white bear for the last ten seconds. If you truly wanted to stop thinking of a white bear, you would be better off allowing yourself to think of one and then after a while the thought would naturally go away—just as every thought eventually does. The attempt to actively suppress a thought, to fight it and block it, keeps it fresh and intense. Similarly, emotions such as anxiety, anger, or envy intensify when we try to suppress them, when we try to fight them and block their natural flow. An Optimalist understands that and allows himself to experience painful emotions, knowing that by doing so these emotions are more likely to weaken and fade away.

When I began teaching, one of the most difficult challenges I faced was overcoming my anxiety about public speaking. As an introvert and a Perfectionist, I felt so much anxiety during lectures that, quite beyond the fact that I was sure everyone in the audience could hear my heart pounding, I found it difficult to remember what I wanted to say, and I could hardly speak because my mouth was so dry. My initial response was to attack the anxiety head-on, to simply refuse to tolerate this disruptive emotion. To my chagrin, the emotion intensified. It was only when I stopped trying to suppress my anxiety and began to allow myself to feel nervous—when I accepted my anxiety and gave it permission to be—that it started to weaken.

Genuine acceptance of emotions cannot be conditional or instrumental. If the only reason we give ourselves the permission to be human is as a means to an end—so that we can succeed more, for instance—then we are engaging in what I think of as *pseudo-acceptance*. And this does not work. In the case of my anxiety about public speaking, it would not have helped if I had told myself something along the lines of, "OK, let me do this acceptance of anxiety thing so that I can deliver a perfect lecture with perfect calm." We have to *truly* accept our emotions for what they are and truly be willing to live with them. This means that we have to accept painful emotions even when they persist beyond our wants or wishes. Genuine acceptance is about accepting that we are upset and then accepting that we might not feel better even though we accept that we are upset. The capacity for true acceptance is at the heart of the difference between the Perfectionist and the Optimalist.

## Acceptance

One of the key messages of the Kabbalah, the teachings of Jewish mysticism, is that one must have "the will to accept, for the purpose of influence." The word *kabbalah* itself means "acceptance," and in this context the word *influence* means "the creation of spiritual and physical affluence." When we fully accept reality—the good and the bad, the pleasurable and the painful—we can create and spread affluence; when we accept rather than resist, we become a pipeline, a conduit, through which wisdom and goodness can flow. While this notion might sound mystical—coming, after all, from Jewish mystical tradition—the message it conveys is, in essence, scientific.

Francis Bacon, philosophical father of the scientific revolution, wrote that "Nature to be commanded must be obeyed." Bacon, like the Kabbalah, argues that to create affluence, to channel nature's potential for our own purposes, we must first accept reality and work with it rather than reject it. It is only when we accept nature's laws and processes—when we come to terms with their existence rather than perceive them as alterable—that we can make productive use of them. The birth of the scientific revolution, which in turn gave rise to the industrial revolution and to unprecedented material affluence, came about when people followed Bacon's advice and obeyed nature—accepting the natural world for what it is rather than rejecting its laws and replacing them with mystical beliefs.

Bacon's advice applies as much to our inner lives as it does to the world around us. The Perfectionist pays a heavy price when he disregards his nature, when he refuses to accept the reality of painful emotions and rejects them. The Optimist is more likely to enjoy psychological affluence, to derive satisfaction from his life, because he acknowledges nature and accepts that painful emotions are an inevitable part of reality. In the same way that scientists were only able to make significant advances in technology by accepting the laws of physical nature—of gravity and thermodynamics, for instance—we too can only grow and lead richer, fuller lives by accepting the laws of human nature. And, like it or not, painful emotions are part of that nature.

## Healing the Pain

If we inject water into a clogged pipeline, the pressure will increase a great deal more than if the water is allowed to flow freely through a clear pipeline; similarly, if we allow painful emotions to flow through us naturally, freely, the pressure eases and they eventually subside. A continuous buildup of water pressure can lead the pipeline to break down and burst; a buildup of unreleased painful feelings can lead to emotional breakdown. While this is a risk that Perfectionists face, Optimalists do not place themselves in a situation where emotional pressure can rise uncontrollably over a long period of time. Instead of denying their pain and fighting it, they accept it; rather than condemning themselves for feeling anxious, they accept their anxiety and allow it to flow through them and take its course.

Philosopher Alan Watts, who did much to bring Zen to the West, wrote, "The difference of the adept in Zen from the ordinary run of men is that the latter are, in one way or another, at odds with their humanity." When we stop resisting who we are and what we feel, we drop the heavy burden of an endless, hopeless battle against our humanity.

**TIME-IN** In what ways do you find yourself at odds with your humanity?

Viktor Frankl proposed the technique of *paradoxical intentions* as a method for dealing with stress or anxiety. Frankl suggested that rather than trying to rid ourselves of our anxiety, we should try to induce further anxiety—we should encourage ourselves to feel more anxious, more nervous. As a result, because we allow the anxiety to flow freely through us, it weakens. This particular technique has helped me a great deal in dealing with my anxiety about public speaking. Instead of fighting it, I called forth more of it! I exhorted myself to be more anxious, more nervous. Paradoxically, this calmed me down.

Therapist and researcher David Barlow and his colleagues propose a similar approach to dealing with stress and anxiety: *worry exposure*. Clients struggling with excessive anxiety levels are asked to imagine the worst-case scenario relating to the cause of their concerns. They are given the following instructions: "It is essential that you imagine the worst event happening and concentrate on it as hard as you can. Do not avoid this thought or image, since avoiding it will defeat the whole purpose of the exercise."[2] First, clients are encouraged to fully experience the emotion and the discomfort that comes with the imagined scenario. Only then do they proceed to the second stage, which is to calm down and deal with the irrationality of their thoughts. While their anxiety initially intensifies as a result of worry exposure, anxiety levels soon drop below what they were originally. Clients are often amazed by how quickly and naturally their anxiety abates.

Matthieu Ricard, Buddhist monk and scientist, notes that "the more you look at anger, the more it disappears beneath one's very eyes, like the frost melting under the morning sun. When one genuinely looks at it, it suddenly loses its strength."[3] The same applies to envy, sadness, anxiety, hate, and other painful emotions.

We are all born with innate abilities to heal ourselves. We are able to fight off germs, to repair broken bones, to grow new skin. In order to heal physically, we need to give the natural healer in us the time it needs to do its work. We have a similar mechanism to heal psychological injuries. But in addition to time, psychological healing requires that we shift our attention to our emotional pain and keep it there. Just as we don't need professional assistance to heal from every bruise or scrape, in many cases it is sufficient to allow our internal psychological healer to function without calling in external support.

Oxford psychologist Mark Williams and his colleagues have shown that intentionally, mindfully focusing on the physical manifestations of depression helps in overcoming depression and in reducing the likelihood of relapsing after recovery. In fact, the researchers found that often "trying to get rid of depression in the usual problem solving way, trying to 'fix' what's 'wrong' with us, just digs us in deeper."[4] The solution to many—not all, but many—of our psychological afflictions lies not in the fixing/doing mode but in the accepting/being mode.

It is this mode that allows the natural healer to do its magic. As Williams writes, "With the shift from trying to ignore or eliminate physical discomfort to paying attention with friendly curiosity, we can transform our experience." Accepting our emotions means looking at them in a benign way, welcoming them as part of our nature, and thus as something interesting and worthy. For me, simply taking mental note of my anxiety before a lecture without trying to change it, becoming mindful of the parts of my body where the anxiety manifested itself without actively trying to make the discomfort go away, decreased my anxiety.

It is important to distinguish between accepting painful emotions and ruminating on them. Acceptance involves gently *being* with the emotion; rumination involves obsessively thinking about the emotion. Obsessing about the emotion or the event that led to it is unproductive and unhealthy, and may intensify, rather than dissolve, the emotion: "rumination is part of the problem, not part of the solution."[5]

This is not to suggest that analyzing or thinking about an emotion or its causes can't help us feel better—it certainly can. However, rather than having thoughts playing in an endless loop in our heads (ruminating), we would be better off expressing our thoughts verbally or in writing.[6] Keeping a personal journal in which we express our thoughts and feelings can yield significant benefits. In a set of experiments, psychologist James Pennebaker demonstrated that students who on four consecutive days spent twenty minutes writing about difficult experiences were ultimately happier and physically healthier.[7] Expressing our thoughts and sharing our feelings in conversation with someone we trust can be at least as helpful as expressing them in writing.

While we do not need to scream as we are walking on Main Street or shout at our boss who makes us angry, we should, when possible, provide a channel for the expression of our emotions. We can talk to a friend about our anger and anxiety, write in our journal about our fear or jealousy, join a support group of people who are struggling with issues similar to ours, and, at times, in solitude or in the presence of someone who cares about us, allow ourselves to shed a tear—of sorrow or of joy.

**TIME-IN**   What are some of the outlets in your life for the expression of painful emotions? Are there people you trust? Are there people with whom you can build trust? Do you keep a journal?

## The Range of Human Emotions

The best advice that my wife, Tami, and I received when David, our first child, was born came from our pediatrician. "Over the next few months," he said, "you're going to experience a whole range of emotions, often to the extreme. You're going to experience joy and awe, frustration and anger, happiness and irritation. This is normal. We all go through it." Was he right! While there certainly were moments of joy, there were difficult moments, too. For example, when David was a month old, I started to feel some envy toward him. Why? Because for the first time since Tami and I had started dating, her attention was focused on someone else more than on me. But then five minutes after feeling envy, I would experience the most intense love toward David. My initial reaction was to label myself a hypocrite, to question the authenticity of my love: how could my feelings of love for him be real if at the same time I also envied him? And then our pediatrician's words came to mind, reminding me that it was natural to feel what I was feeling, essentially giving me the permission to be human.

The doctor's advice helped in two related ways. First, because I recognized and accepted—rather than rejected and suppressed—my feeling of envy, it gradually subsided and lost its hold. Second, I was able to experience and enjoy the feeling of love much more intensely, without it being marred by feelings of guilt or disingenuousness.

Acceptance is a prerequisite for a healthy emotional life. When we accept our emotions, when we welcome everything that is human about us, we open up a space within which we can feel. Closing off the emotional valve to the flow of painful emotions inevitably restricts future flow of positive emotions, too. The same system is used for the flow of all emotions—positive and painful—and if we block the flow of one emotion, it affects our ability to experience other emotions. When I refuse to accept that I am upset after I make a mistake, I hinder my ability to experience joy when something good happens to me. When I do not recognize my anger toward my partner, I limit my capacity to love. When I reject my fear, I stifle my courage. When I do not give myself the permission to experience envy, I undermine my generosity. In the words of psychologist Abraham Maslow, "By protecting himself against the hell within himself, he also cuts himself off from the heaven within."

No person can enjoy a "perfect" emotional life, an unbroken chain of positive emotions. Trying to lead that kind of life by rejecting painful emotions when they arise only increases suffering. For optimal human functioning—for us to enjoy the best possible life—we need to give ourselves the permission and the space to experience and express the full range of human emotions.

## Acceptance and Resignation

Accepting an emotion does mean resigning to it. Nathaniel Branden explains:

> The willingness to experience and accept our feelings carries no implication that emotions are to have the last word on what we do. I may not be in the mood to work today; I can acknowledge my feelings, experience them, accept them—and then go to work. I will work with a clearer mind because I have not begun the day with self-deception. Often, when we fully experience and accept negative feelings, we are able to let go of them; they have been allowed to have their say and they relinquish center stage.[8]

Along similar lines, psychologist Jon Kabat-Zinn notes, "Acceptance of the present moment has nothing to do with resignation in the face of what is happening. It simply means a clear acknowledgment that what is happening is happening."[9] In fact, acceptance is the first step we need to take if we are concerned with change. Carl Rogers, founder of the client-centered school of therapy, points out that "the curious paradox is that when I accept myself just as I am, then I can change."[10] For example, if I am too sensitive to other people's opinions of me and want to change that about myself, condemning myself each time I overreact is unlikely to prove helpful. Accepting myself, sensitivity and all, is more likely to help me become more resilient. When I accept the emotion—when I accept myself—that's when I am in the best mind-set and heart-set to change.

Accepting our emotions does not imply that we like them but rather that we are giving ourselves the permission, the space, and the freedom to feel as we do. Accepting emotions also does not mean that we accept the behaviors that might spring from them. I can experience envy toward my child (an emotion) and yet still act with kindness toward him (my behavior); I can experience anxiety before a lecture and still choose to teach. This is the essence of active acceptance as opposed to passive resignation.

## Active Acceptance

When the CEO of a company I had been consulting for expressed interest in a leadership seminar, I asked one of my friends, an expert on leadership and an excellent speaker, for help. My friend and I planned the seminar together and then shared the teaching between us. Watching my friend interact with my client, seeing how captivated the participants were by his eloquence, I began to regret having asked him to join me. I was jealous.

I was so upset with myself for feeling the way I did that I hardly slept for three nights. How could I feel jealousy toward a friend? How could I feel regret over asking him to work with me when I knew that everyone involved—myself and the participants—had learned so much from him? Finally, I decided to tell him what I felt—part confession, part request for advice. He told me that he, too, had felt jealous when he observed me teach. On that day, and for a long time after, we discussed our respective experiences of jealousy. Simply talking about it made us feel better and brought us closer together. Our only conclusion, though, was that jealousy is natural and, to some extent, unavoidable.

Certain feelings are inescapable. No person is free from the experience of jealousy or fear or anxiety or anger. The real question is not whether we experience these feelings—we all do—but what we decide to do about them. Our first choice is whether to reject or accept our emotional reaction, whether to suppress or acknowledge that which is. Our second choice is whether to act on our initial impulse (for instance, to stop collaborating with people we're jealous of) or whether to go beyond it (create as many alliances with talented people as we possibly can). The second choice is made significantly easier if, first, we choose to accept our feelings: negative emotions intensify and are more likely to control us if we try to suppress them.

If we refuse to accept that we can be jealous of a friend, we are likely to behave badly toward him and then rationalize our behavior. If we do not accept that we are afraid to ask someone out, we are likely to avoid that person and then convince ourselves that we didn't really like her anyway. Had I denied that my feelings toward my friend were driven by jealousy, I would have looked for an alternative explanation for my discomfort around him. We are creatures of feeling and reason, and once we feel a certain way, we have the need to find a reason for our feeling. Rather than dealing with the real reason for my emotional reaction, rather than admitting to feelings of which I did not approve, I would probably have justified my discomfort around him by finding fault with him. To avoid thinking ill of ourselves, we often condemn the people we have wronged.

There is another potential harm in suppressing unwanted thoughts or feelings. In their work on "defensive projection," psychologist Leonard Newman and his colleagues have shown that "when people are motivated to avoid seeing certain faults in themselves, they contrive instead to see those same faults in others."[11] These unwanted thoughts and feelings become "chronically accessible"—just as a white bear becomes chronically accessible when we attempt to suppress the thought of it—and we see them everywhere around us, in other people, even when they are not really there.

We pollute our environment with our unacknowledged thoughts and feelings. Had I denied my jealousy toward my friend, I would have been more likely to blame him and others for being jealous. At the end of the process that started with suppressing my real feelings, I would have harmed myself, my friend, our relationship, and potentially others as well.

Whenever we suppress a painful emotion we—as well as those around us—pay a price. If, for example, we do not acknowledge our anger within a romantic relationship, we will most likely "project" that anger outward—see it in our partner or in others even when it is not there—and inadvertently end up hurting our partner and our relationship. If, at work, we do not act authentically—if we do not speak up when we know we should, or we say things we don't believe just to impress others—and then refuse to acknowledge our behavior, we will begin to see inauthenticity all around us and unjustly criticize others. It is when we accept our feelings—those we like and those we don't—that we open up the possibility of acting nobly.

**TIME-IN** When in your life have you felt, or do you feel, jealousy or envy? Observe the feeling, accept it without trying to change it, and then commit to behaving in ways that you deem noble.

What would your life look like if you refuse to accept the law of gravity? For starters, you may not survive for long if you ignore the fact that things, people being no exception, fall when left in midair. But even if you do survive, imagine the frustration, the feelings of inadequacy that would dominate your daily existence. So, though we may not like the law of gravity, we accept it and learn to live within its constraints.

Painful emotions are as much part of human nature as the law of gravity is part of physical nature, and yet most people accept and embrace the latter while rejecting and denying the former. To lead a fulfilling, healthy life, we need to accept our emotions in the same way we accept other natural phenomena. When we accept physical nature—the law of gravity, for instance—as a given, we can design machines that fly at high speeds or create games that celebrate the physical law (imagine the Olympics without gravity). Similarly, if we accept human nature—the existence of painful emotions, for instance—we are much better able to design the kind of life we want for ourselves. Would you buy an airplane designed by an engineer who does not accept the laws of nature? Why not apply the same standards when it comes to human nature? Why settle for less when your own happiness is at stake?

## Morality and Emotions

We are not doing ourselves justice when we reproach ourselves for feeling a certain way. Moral evaluation—the judgment as to whether something is good or bad—presupposes choice. And where there is no choice, there are no grounds for moral evaluation. For example, we may not like the law of gravity, but gravity in and of itself is neither good nor bad—it simply is. Similarly, we may not like feeling fear, but the feeling itself is neither good nor bad—it, too, simply is. Feeling jealousy toward my friend does not make me a bad friend; if, however, I jeopardize my friend's success because of my jealousy, then I am a bad friend. Feeling anxious when I meet a person I would very much like to go out with says nothing about my courage—running away from something I very much want because I fear being turned down does.

In an interview with Oprah Winfrey, Nelson Mandela illustrated the value of active acceptance. When describing his own and others' feelings toward the apartheid regime, he said:

> Our emotion said the white minority is an enemy, you must never talk to them, but our brain said, if you don't talk to them your country will go up in flames and for many years to come this country will be covered with rivers of blood. So we had to reconcile this conflict and our talking with the enemy was the result of the domination of the brain over emotion.

Mandela openly acknowledged his feelings. "When I think about the past, the types of things they did, I feel angry, but again that is my feeling. The brain always dominates." Mandela did not pretend that he had warm feelings toward those who imprisoned him for twenty-seven years and who oppressed millions of people because of the color of their skin. The feelings of bitterness, of anger, and of revenge were there, they were real, and acknowledging their reality helped him think, and act, with reason. By first choosing to accept these emotions and then choosing to behave benevolently toward his former oppressors, Mandela was able to lead South Africa through its most challenging period of transformation.

We all have an image of our ideal self, an elaborate construct of the kind of person we would like to be. While it is not always possible to *feel* as this constructed self would (fearless and compassionate at all times, for example), we can act in accordance with its ideals (courageous, generous, and so on).

Active acceptance is about recognizing things as they are and then choosing the course of action we deem appropriate and worthy of ourselves. It is about recognizing that at every moment in our life we have a choice—to be afraid and yet to act courageously, to feel jealous and yet to act benevolently, to accept being human and act with humanity.

**TIME-IN** Which painful emotions do you tend to have trouble accepting? Once you accept these emotions, what would be the most appropriate action to take?

## Emotional Growth

It is impossible to describe the pain that follows the loss of someone we loved. The person left behind to mourn is often unable to contemplate life without the deceased. However, what happens next varies drastically among individuals. Some people never recover from the loss. Others move on, after a period of grief, and are able to function as they did before, in terms of both their actions and their emotions. Finally, there are those who experience what Lawrence Calhoun and Richard Tedeschi call posttraumatic growth; the loss transforms them in profound ways—they appreciate life more, their relationships improve, and they become more resilient.[12]

Bonny died on December 19, 1997, two weeks before her thirtieth birthday. Her flight, Silk Air 185 from Jakarta, crashed at 5 P.M.—one hour before its estimated time of arrival in Singapore's Changi International Airport and two hours before she was supposed to call me in my room, in a hotel on Beach Road.

When I hadn't heard from Bonny by 7:15 P.M., I called the airport to find out whether the flight was delayed. I began to worry when I was transferred from one operator to another. Finally, a woman's voice broke the pattern: "To find out more about the flight, you have to come to the airport."

"Why?" I asked.

"To find out more," the operator repeated, "you have to come to the airport." I called the airport again and was told the same thing by another operator.

"I can't come to the airport," I lied. "I am calling from Jakarta."

In a matter-of-fact tone, she said, "We lost radar contact with the plane over two hours ago. We have no further information."

I fell to the floor, too weak to live. And then I screamed. I never screamed like that before or since.

The pain, especially for the first eight months, was unbearable. It was so overwhelming that I thought it would never end. How could it, when it felt more concrete—more real and permanent— than anything else in my life?

And yet eventually the pain did subside, and I gradually moved on. How did this happen? How does emotional healing—let alone emotional growth—take place, and what does the recovery process look like? We can gain some insight into the process of emotional development by looking at the process of cognitive development.

The theory of *cognitive disequilibration* explains mental development using bricks as a metaphor. Each new piece of information or knowledge that we gain is an additional brick, which we lay on an existing one. The brick structure gets taller over time and eventually becomes unstable. It sways from side to side, loses its balance, its equilibrium, and finally crashes. Disequilibration takes place: the old construction collapses, the bricks fall to the ground, and the wreckage becomes the foundation for a new structure. This foundation is wider than the previous one and thus able to support a taller structure. As we continue developing, more bricks are placed on top of the wider foundation until this structure, too, ultimately becomes unstable. The structure collapses, again a wider foundation is formed, and so on.

This, too, is the nature of eureka experiences—the aha! moments when we have an insight. These moments are usually the culmination of much effort over a long period of time. As we learn more, we are adding more bricks to our cognitive construct. Eventually, the cognitive construct loses its equilibrium, collapses, and then reemerges as a new, stronger foundation that is able to support a wider, taller structure. The eureka experience occurs when the existing structure of knowledge collapses and the fragments of knowledge come together in a different way—as a new insight from which we can learn and upon which we can build.

A similar process occurs on a greater scale with respect to entire fields of human knowledge. According to philosopher of science Thomas Kuhn, a paradigm shift occurs within a scientific discipline when the old paradigm is no longer able to contain and satisfactorily explain the new knowledge that has accumulated.[13] Like a brick tower, the old paradigm crumbles to form a new foundation, which then becomes the genesis of a new paradigm. The process repeats itself when the new paradigm, in its turn, is no longer able to contain the accumulation of knowledge, and once again the foundation for a new paradigm is formed out of the wreckage of the old.

The disequilibration model applies as much to the realm of emotions as it does to the realm of thought. Each emotional experience is like a new brick that is placed on top of our existing emotional structure. After a while, the structure becomes too high for its foundation, the bricks collapse, and emotional disequilibration takes place. A new foundation is formed, one that is wider at its base, and therefore more solid and able to bear a greater load.

Returning to the metaphor of the pipeline through which all of our emotions flow, a wider foundation is parallel to a wider pipeline, one that has a larger capacity for the flow of emotions, one that is able to effectively handle larger quantities of feelings, both painful and pleasurable.

In *The Prophet*, Khalil Gibran describes how each time we experience sorrow, our capacity for joy increases:

> Your joy is your sorrow unmasked.
> And the selfsame well from which your laughter rises was
>     oftentimes filled with your tears.
> And how else can it be?
> The deeper that sorrow carves into your being, the more joy
>     you can contain.[14]

Following Bonny's death I went through emotional disequilibration, breaking down and then slowly building up again. Extreme emotional experiences can lead to accelerated emotional disequilibration and hence to post-traumatic growth.

Emotional disequilibration does not happen only as a result of negative experiences. Every time we allow ourselves to feel, we grow. This is why peak experiences—moments of bliss, ecstasy, supreme joy—can transform us.[15] For example, some women report that the experience of childbirth changed them forever, that they became more self-confident, happier, calmer, or generous as a result. Aesthetic experiences, such as reading a novel or looking at a painting, can expand our emotional understanding of the world and open our emotional floodgates. Profound religious experiences can also alter the way we see the world around us and lead us to a spiritual depth that we never attained before. It's important to realize, however, that these extreme positive and negative emotional experiences provide the *opportunity* for growth; they do not automatically induce growth. To seize this opportunity, we need to openly embrace the emotions that these experiences elicit.

There are more parallels between emotional and cognitive growth. Dogmatism is about closed-mindedness, about rigidly holding on to one's own position and ideas, without consideration for other points of view. Cognitive disequilibration—intellectual growth, a eureka experience, a paradigm shift—is less likely to take place if we are dogmatic, if we are unwilling to open ourselves up to different ways of understanding and seeing the world. There is also what we might think of as *emotional dogmatism*, which is about closing our heart, not being open to the full range of emotions that our experiences generate in us. Emotional disequilibration is unlikely to take place if we are emotionally dogmatic, unwilling to allow ourselves the experience of strong emotions.

The Perfectionist, rigid and unyielding, is an emotional dogmatist; he suppresses painful feelings in his ongoing attempt to sustain the unbroken flow of positive emotions. Cognitive dogmatism (closed-mindedness) and emotional dogmatism (closed-heartedness) lead to the same outcome: stagnation.

## Healthy Grieving

In his work on bereavement, Colin Murray Parkes describes how widows who do not express their emotions following the death of their husbands suffer from longer-lasting and more severe physical and psychological symptoms than widows who "break down" after their loss. In the words of Marcel Proust, "We are healed of a suffering only by expressing it to the full." James Pennebaker reports on studies that show that "the more people talked to others about the death of their spouse, the fewer health problems they reported having." After some time, while they continue to experience pain—and continue to accept it—they are able to go on with their lives.

The most extensive work on grief was conducted by therapist William Worden, who suggested that the process of mourning comprises four stages: accepting the reality of the loss, working through the pain of grief, adjusting to life without the deceased, and moving on.[16] Not going through the four stages (either sequentially or with some overlap) could thwart the healing process and lead to long-term complications.

The first stage has to do with one of the common responses to loss, which is denial, either by refusing to come to terms with the fact that the person is gone or by belittling the value of the relationship with the person who passed. For healthy recovery, the person who experienced loss has to accept reality: both the fact that the deceased will not return and the true significance of her relationship with the deceased.

The second stage is working through the pain of grief. Rather than controlling their emotions, pulling themselves together, or being tough, mourners are better off going through the emotions, feeling the pain when it naturally arises, and then expressing it in words and tears. Those who experience loss are often distracted from their pain by well-meaning people who encourage them to stop crying over the dead and get on with their lives or by doctors who prescribe antidepressants. Such strategies usually only prolong the grieving process and the pain. These "strong" mourners fail to recover because, in the words of F. Scott Fitzgerald, "They don't indulge in the cheering luxury of tears."

This stage can take time and requires much patience. There are certain processes that cannot be rushed and need to be allowed to unfold at their natural pace. In Hebrew the word for "patience," *savlanut*, stems from the same root as the word for "suffering," *sevel*. At times, having patience is about enduring suffering.

The third stage involves adjusting to the new reality. A loss could mean having to take over responsibilities of the person who died, having to form a new or revised identity that does not include the role of the deceased in our life, or initiating new relationships to fill the void created by the loss. The adjustments cannot, and should not, come right after the loss, but it is detrimental to the recovery process to avoid making these adjustments.

The final stage, moving on, is difficult, because it may feel like a betrayal of the deceased, as well as of one's own values. How can I continue to enjoy life when she cannot? If I truly loved him, how could life without him possess any significance? The key here is to find an appropriate place in one's heart for the deceased, while simultaneously moving on by investing in meaningful relationships and pleasurable activities.

Looking at Worden's four stages, we see the process of active acceptance. The first two stages are about acceptance: cognitive acceptance in the form of intellectually coming to terms with the loss and emotional acceptance in the form of experiencing the pain. The third and fourth stages—adjusting and moving on—form the active part of the equation.

Grieving does not necessarily need to be restricted to the physical death of a loved one. We can grieve over a meaningful relationship that has soured, over a person we care about deeply who moved away, or over a job that we lost. Going through Worden's four stages of grief can help us heal and grow following loss, regardless of its nature.

When Ralph Waldo Emerson was twenty-seven years old, his beloved wife, Ellen, died. Later, after he remarried and became a father, he lost his two-year-old son. Emerson wrote an essay titled "Compensation," which is a testament to his sense of life and optimism. Here is the last paragraph from the essay, which is essentially about post-traumatic growth, and which gave me hope when I had none:

> And yet the compensations of calamity are made apparent to the understanding also, after long intervals of time. A fever, a mutilation, a cruel disappointment, a loss of wealth, a loss of friends, seems at the moment unpaid loss, and unpayable. But the sure years reveal the deep remedial force that underlies all facts. The death of a dear friend, a wife, brother, lover, which seemed nothing but privation, somewhat later assumes the aspect of a guide or genius; for it commonly operates revolutions in our way of life, terminates an epoch of infancy or of youth which was waiting to be closed, breaks up a wonted occupation, or a household, or style of living, and allows the formation of new ones more friendly to the growth of character. It permits or constrains the formation of new acquaintances and the reception of new influences that prove of the first importance to the next years; and the man or woman who would have remained a sunny garden-flower, with no room for its roots and too much sunshine for its head, by the falling of the walls and the neglect of the gardener is made the banian of the forest, yielding shade and fruit to wide neighborhoods of men.[17]

It has been over ten years since Bonny died. Yesterday, I went running along the Charles River. The New England fall aroused my senses with its hues and warmth. I felt the world, and it was beautiful to me. I marveled at how this existence, that not so long ago was devoid of all luster and purpose, had regained its color and hope.

**TIME-IN** How have you handled loss in the past, whether of a friend, a relationship, or something else that was important to you?

August 2008. David, my four-year-old son, and I are standing in line at the supermarket in Ramat Gan, Israel. Ahead of us a soldier is unloading his groceries onto the counter.

"Why is he a soldier?" asks David.

"Because," I answer, "when he turned eighteen he had to join the military."

David pauses for a minute, looks admiringly at the soldier, and then says, "I also want to be a soldier when I grow up." The soldier pays the cashier and walks off with his bags, smiling at David, who smiles back.

David's eye catches a toy, a green Ninja Turtle with red goggles, hanging next to the counter. "Daddy, can you buy this toy for me?"

"No, David, you already have a toy like it."

Unconvinced, he says, "But mine is old. I want a new one."

Unconvinced, I say, "No."

David begins to cry. There is another man paying the cashier now who looks at David and says, "Soldiers don't cry." David stops crying.

The stranger walks off. David looks up at me, his eyes still moist. I run my hand through his hair. "You can cry if you are sad. Soldiers also cry."

"Then why did the man say that soldiers don't cry?" he asks.

"He made a mistake, sweetie, just like Daddy does sometimes."

# EXERCISES

## ●●●Mindfulness Meditation

Over the last few decades, there has been an increasing amount of research documenting the benefits of mindfulness meditation for physical and mental health. Mindfulness is about being fully aware of whatever it is that we are doing and accepting (as much as possible) the present moment without judgment or evaluation. We are mindful when we focus on the here and now, experience the experience, allow ourselves to feel whatever feelings emerge regardless of whether or not we like what we are feeling. According to John Kabat-Zinn, a leading practitioner and scholar in the field of mind-body medicine, "Mindfulness [involves] the complete 'owning' of each moment of your experience, good, bad, or ugly."[18]

Mindfulness meditation is the *practice* of acceptance. In the same way that understanding in theory what would improve your tennis backhand only takes you so far—you have to actually practice the moves in order to really become good at them—so theorizing about acceptance has its limits.

While the practice of mindfulness meditation itself is simple, implementing it as a regular practice is anything but. For meditation to have a significant impact on the quality of your life, you need to meditate regularly, ideally every day, for at least ten to twenty minutes. However, a session every other day, or even once a week, is certainly better than nothing.

There are many variations on meditation, and attending a class led by an experienced instructor is a good idea. In the meantime, here are instructions for a simple meditation that you can start today.

Sit down, either on the floor or on a chair. Find a position that is comfortable for you, preferably with your back and neck straight. You may close your eyes if it helps you relax and concentrate.

Focus on your breathing. Inhale gently, slowly, and deeply. Feel the air going down all the way to your belly, and then exhale slowly and gently. Feel your belly rise as you breathe in and then falling as you breathe out. For the next few minutes focus on your belly filling up with air as you inhale gently, slowly, and deeply and then being emptied of air as you exhale slowly and gently. If your mind wanders to other places, kindly and calmly bring it back to the rise and the fall of your belly.

You are not trying to change anything. You are simply being.

## ●● Experiencing the Experience

Tara Bennett-Goleman, a therapist who brings together Eastern and Western psychology, writes, "Mindfulness means seeing things as they are, without trying to change them. The point is to dissolve our reactions to disturbing emotions, being careful not to reject the emotion itself."[19] By focusing on a painful emotion, accepting it with an open heart and mind and letting it flow through us, we can help it dissolve, disappear.

For example, if you get extremely nervous in front of an audience, imagine yourself getting onstage; if you lost someone and time has not healed the pain, imagine yourself sitting next to the deceased or saying good-bye to him. You can also bring up certain emotions, from insecurity to sadness, by thinking about them without imagining a particular situation. Once the emotion comes up, just stay with the experience for a few minutes without trying to change it.

Throughout the exercise, to the extent possible, maintain deep, gentle breathing, just as you did for the mindfulness meditation. If your mind wanders, return to whatever it was that you were imagining or experiencing, and continue with the breathing. If tears come up, let them flow; if other emotions, such as anger or disappointment or joy, come up, let them be. If a particular part of your body reacts in a certain way—you get a knot in the throat or an increased heartbeat—you can shift your attention to that part and imagine yourself breathing into it, without trying to change it.

This exercise is about giving yourself the permission to feel, to experience the experience rather than to ruminate on it; it is about accepting the emotions as they are, being with them rather than trying to understand and "fix" them.

# 3

# Accepting Success

If my aim is to prove I am "enough," the project goes on to infinity—because the battle was already lost on the day I conceded the issue was debatable.

—*Nathaniel Branden*

The Greek myth of Sisyphus tells of a man, the most cunning of mortals, who was punished for his pride and disobedience. Sisyphus was condemned by the gods to push a heavy rock up a mountainside and then watch it roll down again, repeating this process for eternity.

Psychologically speaking, the Perfectionist is like Sisyphus. But whereas the punishment of Sisyphus was inflicted by the gods, the Perfectionist's punishment is self-inflicted. No success or conquest, no peak or destination, is ever enough to satisfy the Perfectionist. When he reaches the summit of one mountain or another, when he achieves some form of success, there is no delight, no savoring—only another meaningless journey toward a destination that inevitably disappoints.

The alternative to the Sisyphean archetype is Odysseus, king of Ithaca, who, according to Homer, fought in the war of the Greeks against Troy. After the war was won he wanted to return home to his family and people, but his journey was impeded by Poseidon, the god of the sea. Odysseus struggled against the one-eyed Cyclops, barely escaped the giant man-eating Laestrygonians, and survived the song of the sirens. He was the guest of the enchantress Circe and spent seven years as the captive of the beautiful nymph Calypso. And at the end of his long journey, which was full of despair and delight, gloom and glory, he finally reached home and was reunited with his beloved wife, Penelope.

In psychological terms, Odysseus is an Optimalist. Life is fraught with struggles, difficulties, and disappointments, but the Optimalist is able to find pleasure in the journey without losing his focus on his destination. He learns and grows from adversity, and while he may keep his eye on his eventual goal (in Odysseus's case, returning home), he also savors and takes pleasure in his adventures. And when the Optimalist is rewarded for his struggles, he is fulfilled and grateful—and does not take his success for granted, does not dismiss his accomplishment as insignificant.

The reality that the Perfectionist expects (and therefore creates for himself) is of a Sisyphean battle, a futile struggle. By contrast, the Optimalist's life is an Odyssean epic, a purposeful adventure.

**Figure 3.1**

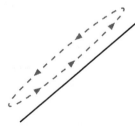

The Perfectionist          The Optimalist

In his essay on the myth of Sisyphus, Albert Camus tries to rescue Sisyphus—and with him all those who perceive their lives as futile and hopeless labor—from his predicament. Camus describes Sisyphus as a tortured, passionate, and absurd hero. But he nevertheless ends his essay on an optimistic and somewhat romantic note:

> I leave Sisyphus at the foot of the mountain! One always finds one's burden again. But Sisyphus teaches the higher fidelity that negates the gods and raises rocks. He too concludes that all is well. This universe henceforth without a master seems to him neither sterile nor futile. Each atom of that stone, each mineral flake of that night-filled mountain, in itself forms a world. The struggle itself toward the heights is enough to fill a man's heart. One must imagine Sisyphus happy.[1]

But can one really imagine Sisyphus happy? Could anyone—other than in literary, poetic moments as Camus, no doubt, found himself in while writing his essay—ever truly invoke Sisyphus's predicament as something romantic and appealing? I doubt it. Sisyphus is not a happy man. Instead, I would suggest, that Camus' writing better describes another Greek hero: one can certainly imagine Odysseus happy.

Sisyphus suffers inordinate pain throughout his journey; Odysseus, too, struggles, but there are moments of joy and delight and learning and growing. When Sisyphus reaches the peak, he is greeted by the bane of his existence; Odysseus at the end of his travels is greeted by the love of his life.

Alasdaire Clayre, the successful Oxford scholar who committed suicide at the age of forty-eight, was a consummate Perfectionist. Though most other people saw Clayre as an astounding success, he saw himself as a failure. A Perfectionist, like Clayre, rejects success, banishes it from his life, either *before* it is attained by setting excessively high standards or *after* it is attained by failing to appreciate it. In other words, the Perfectionist either precludes success from the outset by attempting a slope that is too steep or dismisses success once it is achieved by rolling the rock back down. The Optimist, in contrast, attracts success to his life, first by adopting ambitious yet grounded standards for success (a steep and challenging slope, yet one that can be managed), and second by appreciating success once it is achieved (celebrating and savoring the arrival). It is these two issues—of grounding success and appreciating success—that distinguish between life as a Sisyphean battle and life as an exciting odyssey.

## Grounding Success

When I was growing up, my favorite TV program was a survey of world sports called, after the Olympic motto, "Faster, Higher, Stronger." Every Tuesday evening, for an hour, I was glued to the screen, lamenting when Manchester United edged past Liverpool in the FA Cup final and celebrating the Boston Celtics' victory over the Phoenix Suns in triple overtime, admiring Daley Thompson's superhuman performance in the decathlon and Nadia Comaneci's perfect ten on the parallel bars. Like my heroes on the black-and-white screen, I, too, wanted to run faster, jump higher, and become stronger.

The desire to improve is part of human nature and it serves us well, as it is responsible for personal and societal progress. Taken to the extreme, however, it can harm more than it helps. Psychologist Nathaniel Branden talks of the "nothing is enough" syndrome, the inability that many of us have to be satisfied with what we possess or with who we are. Diane Ackerman describes the syndrome in this way: "Why are we so obsessed with *improving* everything around us: our lawn, our aluminum siding, our chances, ourselves? Regardless of talent, looks, or good fortune, we feel ourselves to be inadequate and in need of some extra genius or flair or energy or serenity."[2] Our constant dissatisfaction condemns us to constant displeasure, for as long as we are human, there is always room for improvement, and even a perfect ten only satisfies us temporarily, until the next competition.

As a squash player, and later as a college student, I felt compelled to live up to a standard of perfection that I had created for myself. And while objectively everything seemed great—academically, on the squash court, and socially—I was in fact constantly stressed, dissatisfied, and frustrated. My academic and other successes did not give me the contentment I sought, because whenever I performed well, the sense of satisfaction was fleeting and I would immediately set my sights on the next goal, the next summit. Nothing was ever enough.

But does this mean that the desire to gain must necessarily produce pain? Should we give up trying to improve ourselves in order to feel adequate as we are? According to William James, father of American psychology, self-esteem is the ratio between success and aspirations, between how well we do and what we aim to do.[3]

$$\text{Self-Esteem} = \frac{\text{Success}}{\text{Aspirations}}$$

In other words, if I aspire to win Olympic gold and actually take home the silver, my self-esteem will drop. But if all I aspire to is participating in the Olympics and I end up winning a bronze medal, my self-esteem will rise. According to James's equation, therefore, if we give up on our desire to improve (in other words, if we keep our aspirations modest), we are more likely to have positive feelings about ourselves. Conversely, if we are ambitious, if we constantly and relentlessly increase our expectations of ourselves, we are doomed to low self-esteem and negative feelings. Though James himself was not one to relax his standards—which was one of the causes to which he attributed his own unhappiness—his theory suggests that we should, at least to a degree, give up on our desire to improve.

But James's equation is only partially correct. While there are times when lowering our aspirations can contribute to our wellbeing, we cannot simply decide to lower them indefinitely and expect to feel better as a result. In fact, low expectations are just as much a prescription for unhappiness as unrealistically high ones. If our aspirations are unrealistically high and we refuse to accept our limitations, we become unhappy; if our aspirations are unrealistically low and we refuse to acknowledge our true potential, not only our success but also our happiness is compromised. "If you deliberately plan on being less than you are capable of being," says Abraham Maslow, "then I warn you that you'll be unhappy for the rest of your life." So how do we know whether, when, and to what extent to lower our aspirations? And how do we know when to raise them? The answer is that we need to be guided by reality.

In his research on flow, psychologist Mihaly Csikszentmihalyi demonstrates that for peak experience and peak performance—for happiness and success—we need to engage in activities that are neither too easy nor too difficult. If we are not challenged enough, we become bored; if our aspirations are overly ambitious, we become anxious.[4] Edwin Locke and Gary Latham, considered the leading researchers in the area of goal setting, summarize thirty-five years of empirical evidence in their field: "The highest or most difficult goals produced the highest levels of effort and performance. . . . Performance leveled off or decreased only when the limits of ability were reached or when commitment to a highly difficult goal lapsed."[5] So while stretching ourselves, pushing ourselves to greater heights, can be a good thing, there is a point beyond which it becomes a bad thing. *We need to accept that our limits are real.*

In his book *Good to Great*, Jim Collins tells the story of Admiral James Stockdale, the highest-ranking American prisoner of war in Vietnam.[6] Known for his unbreakable character and resilience, Stockdale described the two defining characteristics of American captives who were most likely to survive the brutal conditions of a Vietnamese prison. First, they openly faced and accepted rather than ignored or dismissed the harsh facts of their predicament. Second, they never stopped believing that they would someday get out. In other words, while they did not run away from reality, accepting the brutal truths about their current conditions, they never lost hope that all would work out well in the end. By contrast, both those who believed that they would never get out and those who believed that they would be freed within an unrealistically short period of time were unlikely to survive.

Finding that balance between, on the one hand, high hopes and great expectations and, on the other, harsh reality, applies to healthy goal setting in general. The Perfectionist has expectations of himself and sets himself targets that cannot be met; the Optimalist sets high goals that are difficult but attainable. While there is no simple technique to identify which goals are realistic and capable of inspiring us, psychologist Richard Hackman suggests that "the right place to be for maximum motivation is wherever it is that you have a fifty-fifty chance of success."[7]

**TIME-IN** Think of a goal that you already have, and, if necessary, modify it so that it is both attainable and challenging. Think of at least one new goal that will stretch you and yet will be realistic.

## The Good-Enough Life

In the beginning, Man went to work in the morning and came home in the evening, while Woman stayed at home and took care of the house, the children, and Man. Then World War II came, and Man left for Europe or the Pacific. Woman was asked to support the war effort and spend some time in the factory, just temporarily, until Man returned. Woman got a taste of Man's world—ate from the forbidden fruit—and she wanted more.

Not only did many women realize that they liked working outside the home, but men conceded—some reluctantly, others gladly—that women could do the work. The world changed, but some things stayed the same. According to Alice D. Domar in her book *Be Happy Without Being Perfect*:

> Even though women worked outside the home, expectations remained high for their roles inside the home. They'd come a long way, baby, but they still had to get dinner on the table, take care of the children, do the laundry, clean the house, remember to send birthday cards to relatives, and keep their husbands sexually satisfied. Society essentially told women that, sure, you can have it all—but if you're going to do it all, you'd better do it well.[8]

Today, while women on average still do a lot more work in the home than men, they are not the only ones who have to do it all and do it well. An increasing number of men are asked, are required—and, yes, sometimes even want—to contribute more in the home and become more involved in the raising of their children.

There was a new world order, one in which both men and women had more privileges and more responsibilities. Unfortunately, though, the feminist revolution, with all its significant achievements, was unable to slow down earth's revolution and extend our days beyond twenty-four hours. So while demands on our time increased significantly, there was no corresponding increase in our time and no corresponding decrease in expectations. In fact, the opposite is the case, as both men and women are expected to work longer hours than they did in the 1950s and 1960s. And yet the message that most women and some men continued to receive from their environment was that not only were they able to do it all, but they could and should do it all. As Domar notes, "Throughout the 1990s and beyond, the media continued to portray complete happiness in all facets of life as an attainable goal."

Man and Woman were officially banished from Pleasantville. In their new world—a world which is more equitable and fair, and also more demanding—can Man and Woman find happiness? The answer, to many, seems to reside in achieving what has come to be called "work-life balance." But what might work-life balance really look like? Given the real-world, twenty-first century constraints of our lives, what would be the optimal way to balance all of our commitments, all the things we have to do, and the things we want to do?

In my twenties, the passionate Perfectionist in me believed that I could indeed have it all. I spent long hours at work, had some social life, and was overall content with my work-life *im*balance. Then I married and had children, my priorities naturally changed, and there was not enough time for anything. I became increasingly frustrated both at home and at work. There was so much more I wanted to accomplish and experience, yet no matter how hard I worked, no matter how much time I spent with my family, I felt I was not doing enough. I was not giving my children as much attention as I wanted, my wife and I did not go out as often as we both wished, I was not getting enough work done, I spent very little time with close friends, and I was falling far short of my ideal in terms of practicing yoga and exercising.

Reflecting on my overall situation, I identified five areas in my life where it was important for me to thrive: as a parent, as a partner, professionally, as a friend, and in the area of personal health. These five areas did not encompass all the things that I cared about in life, but they were the most significant ones to me, the ones that I wanted to spend most of my time on.

To help me find a solution, I looked for role models in each one of these five areas. And while I found people who were doing some of these things well, none of them was a role model in all five areas or even in a majority of them. A manager in one of the organizations I consulted for was thriving at work, but his family life was a wreck. A friend of mine was a wonderful father and did extremely well at work but had very little time with his partner and neglected his health. A couple I knew were accomplished businesspeople who seemed to invest a great deal in one another, but they had no children and wanted none. A former classmate of mine spent ninety minutes at the gym six times a week, but after giving birth to her first child, she decided not to return to work.

These people and others made certain choices. Some of them were satisfied with the choices they had made, but I was not prepared to forgo my commitments to fatherhood, relationship, career, friends, and health. Where did that leave me? I wondered whether in the modern world a person's basic choice was either to essentially give up on an area or two of one's life or to condemn oneself to being frustrated in all areas of life. Was there a third possibility?

There is a third way—the way of the Optimalist. Having found it, I am currently a lot more satisfied with my life as a whole. Reaching this stage took significant readjustment, the adoption of a whole new approach to the way I manage my time and expectations. The first step was to accept the reality that I could not have it all. While it seems obvious that you cannot work fourteen hours a day and remain fit and healthy and be a devoted father and husband, in my perfectionist fantasy world, *nothing* was impossible.

The second step was to ask myself what would be good enough in each of the five areas of my life that were important to me. In a perfect world, I would be spending twelve hours a day engaged in my work; in the real world, nine to five was good enough, even if it meant turning down some opportunities I would have liked to pursue. In a perfect world, I would be practicing yoga for ninety minutes six times a week and spending a similar amount of time at the gym; in the real world, an hour of yoga twice a week and jogging for thirty minutes three times a week was good enough. Similarly, going out with my wife once a week, meeting friends once a week, and spending the remaining evenings at home with my wife and kids was far short of my perfectionist ideal, but it would (have to) do. All this was, as far as I could see, the optimal solution—the best I could do given the various demands and the constraints of my life.

It was a great relief to adopt this new *good-enough* approach. With my revised set of expectations, a fresh sense of satisfaction replaced the old frustration. And, unexpectedly, I found that I was more energized and focused.

While trying to do it all, part of my frustration came from my inability to focus on one thing at a time. For example, I tried to squeeze in work-related phone calls or e-mails when the kids were home because I felt like I didn't get enough work done in the office. While at work, I spent a lot of time on the phone with my wife because we didn't feel satisfied with our conversations, which were constantly disrupted at home. I tried, with little success, to read while on the exercise bike, and my mind wandered constantly to my children when I tried to rest in child's pose on the yoga mat.

I was a "polygamist" of sorts. Feeling unfulfilled in each one of these areas, I tried to make up for it by engaging in more than one activity simultaneously. With the change from a perfectionist fantasy to an optimal, good-enough existence, without my noticing it at first, I also changed to a "serial monogamist"—engaging in each of the different activities exclusively, separately. When I was with my children, I was *with* them, while the computer and phone were off; my friends got my undivided attention when we were together; when my wife and I were on a date, it was our time to share and to love; at work, when writing, my phone and e-mail were off (as they are now) and I was fully focused on the task; and when working out, I was much more likely to enjoy the meditative unity of mind and body. From an unfulfilled polygamist I became a much more satisfied serial monogamist.

The good-enough formula is not fixed. What constitutes good enough varies from person to person. Different people care about different things, and each person has to take the time to identify those areas that are most important to her. For one person, work and friends may be the most important areas, while for another, family and travel will top the list. What constitutes good enough also varies over time—and so requires the fluidity and acceptance of change that are the mark of the Optimalist. For example, as your children grow up and become more independent, they may not be at home as much and you can reallocate some of the time you spend with them. Your job may sometimes require you to put in long hours. A person dear to you may need your help, and you may choose to spend more time with her at the expense of other activities. The basic idea behind the good-enough approach is that we must come to terms with the constraints of our life as a whole and then find the optimal—or near-optimal—allocation of time and effort.

For me, things are far from perfect now, and every now and then I wish I had more time for one activity or another. Sometimes I find that I have to catch up on my e-mail correspondence late at night after the rest of my family has gone to sleep, when I am exhausted. Once in a while, a few days pass without physical exercise. Things are not perfect; but they're just about good enough.

**TIME-IN** What are the areas of your life that are most important to you?

But is good enough *really* good enough? When I first came up with this new approach, I was eager to share it with the students in my leadership seminar. I thought that the good-enough framework could contribute to solving the problem of the work-life balance that we had been discussing. But the reception the idea received from some students—particularly the male students—was not what I had expected. In their eyes it was wholesale compromise.

Part of their reaction, I believe, had to do with their age and stage in life. At twenty, most of them had not really experienced the demands either of family or a professional career, let alone both simultaneously. Beyond that, however, many people of all ages and levels of experience equate the good-enough approach with "doing the bare minimum." My students were all ambitious high-achievers who never in the past had been satisfied with doing the bare minimum in anything they put their minds to.

In fact, however, the good-enough approach actually leads to functioning at one's best—at one's *optimal* level of performance. The narrow approach of the Perfectionist—attempting to attain perfection in every area of life—inevitably leads to compromise and frustration: given the real constraints of time, it really is impossible to do it all. In their book *Just Enough*, Laura Nash and Howard Stevenson note that "you cannot maximize two things if they are tradeoffs, by the very definition of maximizing."[9] Time is a limited resource, and inevitably there are trade-offs to be made when we decide what we want to do with it. However, while we cannot maximize everything, we can optimalize. In contrast to the Perfectionist's narrow view of reality—looking to maximize time spent in each area of life while ignoring the inevitability of trade-offs—the Optimalist looks for the good-enough solution, which is about optimizing the different components of the system. The good-enough approach forgoes unrealistic expectations of perfection and instead opts for the best possible life.

To me, following the good-enough prescription did not mean I couldn't do better—I could and I can. But it does mean that if I am to be realistic, I will have to settle for an optimally balanced life. My values have not changed with the change in approach. My family is the most important part of my life, and I am no less ambitious with regard to my professional life than I was in my twenties. The only difference is that I am taking the road I did not take before—and taking this good-enough road is making all the difference.

# Appreciating Success

Many Perfectionists have trouble appreciating and enjoying success. Some reject success by setting unrealistically high expectations that are unlikely to be attained. Others reject success by dismissing it once it is attained, by never being satisfied with their accomplishments. As I have discussed, the antidote to the unrealistic expectations is grounded success—having realistic standards for success—and, at times, settling for good enough. The antidote to dismissing success by never being satisfied with it is learning to accept and appreciate success.

There are legions of Perfectionists who, despite being wealthy, healthy, famous, and gorgeous, are unhappy. The fact that wealth, prestige, and other measures of success have very little to do with our levels of well-being points to a simple truth, namely that happiness is mainly contingent on our state of mind rather than on our status or the state of our bank account. Once our basic needs are met—needs such as food, shelter, and education—our level of well-being is determined by what we choose to focus on and by our interpretation of external events. Do we view failure as catastrophic, or do we see it as a learning opportunity? Do we see the glass as half empty or half full? Do we appreciate and enjoy what we have, or do we take it for granted and dismiss it?

In their work on resilience, Karen Reivich and Andrew Shatte discuss the notion of tunnel vision, which is about focusing on a small part of reality while essentially ignoring the rest.[10] For example, if there are twenty students attending my lecture and one of them is asleep, focusing my attention exclusively on the sleeping student to the exclusion of all the other students in the class is tunnel vision. Conversely, if nineteen of them are asleep and only one is listening to what I have to say, concluding that my lecture was a success because one student was intellectually engaged is also a form of tunnel vision. Whether leading to a positive or a negative focus, tunnel vision is about detachment from reality. Generally, Perfectionists engage in negative tunnel vision: they dismiss the good in their lives while giving center stage to the bad.

Alice Domar talks of her patients who, to the outside world, seem to have it all and yet are unable to enjoy it all—or any of it, for that matter—because of their perfectionism. The Perfectionist's negative tunnel vision leads her to dismiss her accomplishments, to take them for granted, and then to resume the drudgery of pushing the next heavy rock up the next steep slope. The Optimalist, by contrast, appreciates life as a whole—herself, her successes, and even her failures, which she perceives as opportunities for learning and growing. Consequently, she not only enjoys what she has but also generates more success, more positive events and experiences.

The word *appreciate* has two meanings. The first meaning is "to be thankful," the opposite of taking something for granted. The second meaning is "to increase in value" (as money appreciates in the bank). Combined, these two meanings point to a truth that has been proved repeatedly in research on gratitude: when we appreciate the good in our lives, the good grows and we have more of it. The opposite, sadly, is also true: when we fail to appreciate the good—when we take the good in our lives for granted—the good depreciates.[11]

**TIME-IN** What can you appreciate right now? Make a list of things for which you are grateful.

Psychologists Robert Emmons and Michael McCullough conducted a series of studies in which they asked participants to write down on a daily basis at least five things, major or minor, for which they were grateful.[12] Participants' responses included everything from their parents to the Rolling Stones, from waking up in the morning to God. Putting aside a minute or two every day to express gratitude for one's life turned out to have far-reaching consequences. Compared to the control group, the grateful group not only became more appreciative of life as a whole but also enjoyed higher levels of well-being and positive emotions: they felt happier, more determined, more energetic, and more optimistic. They were also more generous and more likely to offer support to others. Finally, those who expressed gratitude also slept better, exercised more, and experienced fewer symptoms of physical illness.

I have been doing this exercise daily since September 19, 1999 (three years before Emmons and McCullough published their findings), when I heard Oprah tell her viewers to do it—and so I did! From around the time my son David turned three, we have been doing a variation of this exercise together. Every night I ask him, "What was fun for you today?" and then he asks me the same question. My wife and I regularly remind ourselves what we are grateful for in each other and in our relationship. I credit this simple exercise with helping me make the shift from being a Perfectionist, who takes the good for granted, to an Optimalist, who appreciates it. When we make a habit of gratitude, we no longer require a special event to make us happy. We become more aware of good things that happen to us during the day, as we anticipate putting them on our list.

Needless to say, some items on the daily list repeat themselves. For me, God and family make it on the list every night, and beyond that the list contains at least five items (usually more), big or small. One of the challenges of this simple exercise is to maintain freshness—to avoid the trap of turning it into a mindless routine. We do this exercise so that we don't take the good things in our life for granted, but after doing it for a while, the exercise itself can be taken for granted, which of course defeats the purpose.

There are a few measures we can take to counter the potentially numbing impact of repetition. For instance, we could do this exercise on a weekly rather than a daily basis, as Sonja Lyubomirsky suggests.[13] However, there is a downside to turning this into a weekly habit, and that is that the practice of gratitude is less likely to become ingrained. We can attain the best of both worlds—doing it daily while maintaining freshness—if we make a conscious effort to diversify the list or elements of the list. For example, I might focus one day on my daughter Shirelle's smile and the next on a new word she learned. The practice can be varied in other ways, too, such as sharing the list with our partner once in a while or making a drawing of the items for which we are grateful.

Visualizing the items on the list can help. Cognitive psychologist Stephen Kosslyn points out, "Children rely more than older people on imagery in their thinking. . . . Children tend to use imagery more than descriptive representation in their thought."[14] Kosslyn speculates that this reliance on imagery produces the "childlike freshness" that we are more likely to see among the young. Writing down "family" and then visualizing my wife, children, parents, and siblings helps me maintain freshness even though I have expressed gratitude for their presence thousands of times before. We can use our imagination in other ways, such as attempting to reexperience the emotion from earlier in the day when we ate a delicious meal. We savor, or resavor, that which we are grateful for—be it a meal, our child, music we listened to, or the rain.

Generally speaking, the key when expressing gratitude is to be mindful, present. According to Ellen Langer, my dissertation advisor and mentor, we sustain a mindful state by "drawing novel distinctions about the situation and the environment" as opposed to being trapped in "previously constructed categories."[15] Essentially, being mindful is about assuming the Optimalist's cognitive and behavioral flexibility, whereas being mindless is about being stuck in the Perfectionist's rigid mind-set. For example, we are mindful when we think of an original use for a familiar object, when we note a new expression on a familiar face, and so on. Similarly, if when writing down the things for which we are grateful we try to look at them from a new perspective, searching for distinct details or new variations, we remain present in the experience.

A great deal of research illustrates that practicing mindfulness in the way that Langer suggests—by drawing novel distinctions—enhances happiness, creativity, self-acceptance, success, and physical health. When we practice the gratitude exercise mindfully—when we take the time and make the effort to savor the good in our lives—we are benefiting in two ways. First, we become more appreciative, and the good in our lives appreciates. Second, we gain from the exercise of mindfulness, which in itself is beneficial to us.

**TIME-IN** Look around you right now. What have you not noticed before? How could the things you have noticed be seen differently? Are there aspects you did not notice? Is there another perspective from which to see these things?

Expressing gratitude to others—to our parents, teachers, friends, students—is among the most effective ways of raising our own and others' levels of well-being. Martin Seligman introduced the gratitude visit exercise as part of his positive psychology class, asking students to write a letter expressing their appreciation to a person who has helped them in one way or another and then to visit the person and read him the letter. The effect of this exercise, as reported by Seligman and his students, and indeed as confirmed by subsequent research, is remarkable—in terms of the benefit it brought to the giver, to the recipient, and to their relationship.[16]

I have assigned similar exercises in my classes and have on a number of occasions been moved to tears when students reported back. A father hugged his child for the first time in more than a decade, a friendship that had seemingly died years earlier was resurrected, an old coach came away from the meeting looking younger than he had in years. The power of gratitude is immense.

A letter of gratitude is more than just a thank-you note. It requires that you take time to reflect on what the other person means to you, on the ways she has contributed to your life. While there are many ways to express gratitude, the gratitude visit is unique. First, the mere act of writing the letter (whether or not the letter is ever delivered) contributes to the writer's well-being. Second, the time and effort that the writer has invested in writing the letter makes the recipient feel valued. Third, the visit itself provides a personal touch and can intensify the experience. Finally, the existence of an actual letter means the recipient can revisit it and reexperience it; in this way, a single act has long-lasting effects.

A letter of gratitude reminds the recipient of her success, whether as a teacher, friend, parent, coach, or boss. The emotions associated with giving or receiving such a letter are often no less positive and no less intense than emotions we experience following our greatest accomplishments. As a result, our understanding of success expands to include accomplishments that we would have previously taken for granted and dismissed. A teacher may look at her day-to-day work as ordinary and uninspiring; a letter of gratitude from a student can inspire her and help her realize what a difference her work has made and how successful she really has been.

A single letter of gratitude boosts our levels of well-being, but for the writer this spike is usually temporary. For letters of gratitude and gratitude visits to have a more lasting effect, they would have to become a habit. Writing a weekly, biweekly, or even a monthly letter can do a great deal of good.

**TIME-IN** Think of a person whom you appreciate. What do you appreciate in that person? What are you grateful for?

Being thankful for what we have, not taking our accomplishments for granted, will bring more success into our lives. If more people were to express gratitude to others—to their parents, colleagues, partners, teachers, and friends—then the good in the world would appreciate. As Cicero pointed out, "Gratitude is not only the greatest of virtues, but the parent of all others."

# EXERCISES

## ●● Good Enough

Make a list of the most important areas in your life. You can use categories such as professional, family, romantic, friends, health, travel, hobby, art, or others. First note under each category what you would *ideally* like to do and how much time you would *ideally* like to spend. Then, for each category distinguish between the part that you can give up and the part that you see as indispensable. Write down the indispensable activities under your *good-enough* list. For example, under work, your ideal might be eighty hours a week. Given other constraints and desires, that may not be realistic. Good enough for you might be fifty hours a week. Ideal in the friendship category might be meeting friends every night after work; good enough might be two evenings a week. In a perfect world, you would play fifteen rounds of golf a month; three rounds a month, though, might be good enough.

| Category | Ideal (Perfect) | Good Enough (Optimal) |
|---|---|---|
| Work | Eighty-hour weeks | Fifty-hour weeks |
| Friends | Daily get-togethers | Two weekly get-togethers |
| Golf | A round every other day | Three rounds a month |

After you introduce these changes, revisit your list once in a while. Are you trying to do too much? Too little? What has changed? Is the compromise that you have made in one area of your life making you unhappy? Could you do a little more there and perhaps a little less in another area? There are no easy formulas for finding the optimal balance. Moreover, our needs and wants change over time, as we change and as our situation changes. Be attentive to your inner needs and wants, as well as to the external constraints.

## Gratitude Visit

Write a letter to someone you appreciate, expressing your gratitude to him or her. Refer to particular events and experiences, to things that he or she did for which you are grateful. There is benefit just in writing the letter, but the value is increased if you actually send the letter or, better yet, deliver it in person.

Write down the names of at least five other people you appreciate, and commit to actual dates when you will be writing and delivering gratitude letters to them.

# Accepting Reality

Two and two do make four. Nature doesn't
ask your advice. She isn't interested in your
preferences or whether or not you approve of her
laws. You must accept nature as she is with all
the consequences that that implies.

—*Fyodor Dostoyevsky*

This chapter is about the philosophy of perfectionism and more
specifically about metaphysics, the branch of philosophy that
studies the nature of reality. Metaphysics is important to the
study of perfectionism because underlying many of the Perfectionist's characteristics is the rejection of reality—whether it is in
the form of failure, painful emotions, or success.

We can trace perfectionism's intellectual roots to Plato, the
father of Western philosophy. Aristotle, Plato's student, broke
away from his teacher and preached realism and thus became the
de facto father of optimalism. The distinction between Platonic
and Aristotelian philosophy is captured in Raphael's painting *The
School of Athens*, in which Plato points to the sky and Aristotle
points to the ground. While tomes have been written about their
different approaches to philosophy, I would like to focus on their

*Plato, the Perfectionist (left), and Aristotle, the Optimalist*

different approaches to psychology, specifically as it relates to perfectionism. Plato the Perfectionist is pointing to the dwelling place of the gods, to the supernatural, to the perfect. Aristotle the Optimalist is pointing to *this* world, to the natural, to the real.

According to Plato, the primary building blocks of reality are *forms*—perfect archetypes, ideal models—from which particular objects arise. Plato argues that although we may think we live in the real world, we do not; we are like cave dwellers who are facing away from the entrance to the cave, bound and unable to turn around or leave. The real world, the world of perfect forms, exists outside the cave, where a fire burns and projects the shadows of the forms onto the wall of the cave for us to see. In modern-day terms, we spend our lives locked up in a movie theater, so involved and absorbed in the drama on the big screen that we are oblivious to our actual predicament. Each object that we perceive in our illusory world is a projection of the perfect form that exists in the real world: the horses that we see are mere imperfect projections of the perfect horse, the people that we see around us are not real but imperfect imitations of the perfect human. According to Plato, it is possible to know reality, but only through philosophical contemplation that is not affected by our experiences, our emotions, or what our senses tell us—mistakenly, in his view—about the world.

Unlike Plato, Aristotle's view of reality is not at odds with our experience of the world. While for Plato there are two worlds (the perfect world of forms and the imperfect world we perceive), for Aristotle there is only one world, one reality, which is the world we perceive through our senses. Sense perceptions provide us with experiences, from which we generate forms either as mental images or as words. The mental picture that we have of a horse is derived from our direct or indirect experience of horses. We know what the word *human* means because of our direct or indirect experience of humans.

For Plato, forms are primary, in the sense that the world around us is derived from them. Because we can only know these forms through pure reason that is independent of our experience, thinking precedes experience. For Aristotle, forms are secondary, in the sense that they are derived from the world around us. Because we can only know these forms based on our experience, experience precedes thinking.

The psychological implications of these two very different philosophies are significant. For Plato, our experiences are mere projections of what he considers reality, and they stand in the way of knowledge of the truth (the world of forms). Consequently, if our experience contradicts an idea we hold, we should reject the experience. For example, our experience—which includes our observation of the experiences of others—might teach us that failure is necessary for success. But if our Platonic idea of the path to success—success in its perfect form—is of a straight and unimpeded journey, then we should reject our experience and accept our idea. This is the way Perfectionists form their worldview.

For Aristotle, our experience of the world is fundamental for knowing the truth. Therefore, if experience contradicts a certain idea that we hold, we should reject the idea and not the experience. For example, if we see that the only path to success leads through repeated trial and error, then we should reject the idea—whether it is our own or other people's—that the path to success can be free of failure. This is the way Optimalists form their worldview.

To say "I refuse to feel sad" or "I will not accept failure" is Platonic—an attempt to reject reality by giving precedence to the idea of how we believe we ought to be. To say "I do not like feeling sad, but I accept this emotion as natural" or "I dislike failure, but I accept the fact that some failure is inevitable" is Aristotelian—it acknowledges the primacy of the reality that we experience and observe. Diane Ackerman writes about Plato's impact on perfectionism, "When Plato wrote that everything on earth has its ideal version in heaven, many took what he said literally. But for me the importance of Plato's ideal forms lies not in their truth but in our desire for the flawless." The desire for the flawless condemns us to perpetual displeasure with who we are: "Even the most comely of us feel like eternally ugly ducklings who yearn to be transformed into swans."[1]

**TIME-IN**  What is the appeal of a Platonic philosophy? Why has it had so much influence over the course of history? What is the appeal of Aristotle's ideas? Why have they been so influential?

## The Constrained Vision

Work by Thomas Sowell of the Hoover Institution at Stanford University can help us understand the significance of the Platonic and Aristotelian perspectives. Sowell's work deals mainly with political science, but it has implications for psychology in general and specifically for our understanding of perfectionism and optimalism.

Sowell points out that all political conflicts can essentially be boiled down to a disagreement between two different views of human nature: the constrained view and the unconstrained view.[2] Those who lean toward the constrained view believe that human nature is immutable: it does not change, and we should not waste time and effort trying to modify it. Fashions, technology, landscape, and culture may all change, but human nature is a constant. Human flaws are inevitable, and the best we can do is to accept our nature, its constraints, its imperfectability—and then optimize the outcome based on what we have. Because we cannot change our nature, we must create social institutions that will channel our given nature in the right directions.

In contrast, those who hold the unconstrained view believe that human nature can be changed and improved: solutions exist to every problem, and we should not compromise or be resigned to our imperfections. The role of social institutions is to create systems that will modify our species in the right direction. We therefore sometimes need to work against our nature, to conquer it. Sowell writes, "In the unconstrained vision, human nature is itself a variable and in fact a central variable to be changed."

On the whole, people on both sides have good intentions, but due to a fundamentally different understanding of human nature, they prescribe very different political systems. Those who believe in humanity's constrained nature are typically free-market capitalists, while those who hold the unconstrained view tend to support various forms of utopianism, including Communism.

The capitalist system attempts to channel the individual's self-interest for the common good, and it makes no serious attempt to change people's self-interest or natures. Adam Smith, the Scottish philosopher whose constrained vision gave birth to the free-market economy, wrote, "It is not from the benevolence of the butcher, the brewer, or the baker that we expect our dinner, but from their regard to their own interest. We address ourselves, not to their humanity, but to their self-love, and never talk to them of our own necessities, but of their advantages."

On the other side of the philosophical divide we have Communism, which was inspired by the unconstrained vision of humanity. Communism challenged human nature and sought not to channel it but to change it. In the "New Soviet Person" self-interest would give way to altruism; people would go against their basic instincts, rise above their natural inclinations; human nature would be replaced with superhuman nature. Leon Trotsky, among the leaders of the Bolshevik Revolution, wrote in the early 1920s about the importance of changing man's nature:

> The human species, the coagulated Homo sapiens, will once more enter into a state of radical transformation, and, in his own hands, will become an object of the most complicated methods of artificial selection and psycho-physical training. . . . Man will make it his pur-

pose to master his own feelings, to raise his instincts to the heights of consciousness, to make them transparent, to extend the wires of his will into hidden recesses, and thereby to raise himself to a new plane, to create a higher social biologic type, or, if you please, a superman.

These are inspiring words, and they help to explain how so many people could be seduced by the Communist vision of a better human being and an ideal society. But these ideas and ideals are detached and unrealistic, and they led to the death, murder, and suffering of untold millions of people around the world.

Psychologist Steven Pinker has challenged "the modern denial of human nature," the belief that we are born a blank slate and that everything that we are we acquire from our experiences, from our culture, and from our environment. One of the appeals of the blank slate hypothesis is that our nature can be molded—in other words, made perfect:

> The belief in perfectibility, despite its rosy and uplifting connotation, has a number of dark sides. One of them is the invitation to totalitarian social engineering. Dictators are apt to think: "If people are blank slates, then we damn well better control what gets written on those slates, instead of leaving it up to chance." Some of the worst autocrats of the 20th century explicitly avowed a belief in the Blank Slate. Mao Tse-tung, for example, had a famous saying, "It is on a blank page that the most beautiful poems are written." The Khmer Rouge had a slogan, "Only the newborn baby is spotless."[3]

Adam Smith and other proponents of capitalism were Aristotelian: they believed that there is such a thing as human nature and that government must be constructed around that reality. The Communists were Platonic. They conceived of the ideal form of society, and their objective was to shape the imperfect outside world so that it would reflect the ideal form. Like sculptors, they attempted to carve away the parts of human nature that did not fit the utopian ideal. Plato and those who believe in an unconstrained humanity have a view of what our nature ought to be and strive for this perfection, thus rejecting our *actual* nature; Aristotle and those who believe in a constrained humanity accept human nature as it is and then attempt to make the best, the optimal, use of it.

Clearly, the vision of human nature to which we subscribe has political and societal implications. But its implications on the individual level are no less significant. A Perfectionist subscribes, implicitly or explicitly, to the unconstrained vision of human nature. The refusal to accept painful emotions is a rejection of our nature; it is the belief that human nature can be modified, improved, perfected. While the utopian ideal of Communism was to eradicate the instinct toward self-interest and replace it with altruism, the utopian ideal of the Perfectionist is to eradicate painful emotions, to do away with failure, and to attain unrealistic levels of success.

The Optimalist recognizes and accepts that human nature has certain constraints. We have instincts, inclinations, a nature that some would argue is God-given and others would say has evolved over millions of years. Either way, that nature is not about to change—certainly not in the span of one lifetime—and to make the most of our nature, we need to accept it for what it is. Taking the constraints of reality into consideration, the Optimalist then works toward creating not the perfect life but the best possible one.

The unconstrained view is as detrimental on the individual level as it is on the political, societal one. While optimalism is most certainly not a panacea for all our psychological ills, the quality of life that an Optimalist enjoys is far better than the Perfectionist's. The notion that we can enjoy unlimited success or live without emotional pain and failure may be an inspiring ideal, but it is not a principle by which to lead one's life, since in the long run it leads to dissatisfaction and unhappiness.

## The Law of Identity

Perhaps Aristotle's most important contribution to philosophy and psychology—part of the constrained worldview that he endorsed—is the law of noncontradiction: something cannot be not itself. For example, a "horse" cannot be its contradiction, a "not horse"; a "person" is not a "not person." According to Aristotle, the law of noncontradiction is axiomatic and self-evident and does not require proof: "it is impossible that the same thing can at the same time both belong and not belong to the same object and in the same respect."

From Aristotle's law of noncontradiction follows logically the law of identity, which states that something is itself: a person is a person, an emotion is an emotion, a cat is a cat, a number is a number. The law of identity is the foundation of logic and mathematics and, by extension, of a coherent and meaningful philosophy. Without the law of noncontradiction or the law of identity, says Aristotle, it would be "absolutely impossible to have proof of anything: the process would continue indefinitely, and the result would be no proof of anything whatsoever." We could not even agree on the meaning of a word if we did not accept that something is itself. Even the word *word* or the word *agree* would be meaningless noise if they were not constrained by their identity. It is because we implicitly accept the law of identity that we can communicate and (usually) understand each other.

The law of identity is about recognizing that something is what it is, with all the implications of being what it is. In other words, some things are what they are despite what a person—or the whole world—might wish them to be. Abraham Lincoln once jokingly asked, "How many legs does a dog have if you call the tail a leg?" His answer? "Four. Calling a tail a leg doesn't make it a leg." The law of identity may seem obvious, but it has significant relevance for the way we live our lives. All of us, not just philosophers, must accept the implications of this law: failure to recognize—and act upon the recognition—that something is itself can lead to dire consequences. If, for example, a person treats a truck as something that it's not—as, say, a flower—then this person is in danger of being run over; similarly, if he deals with poison as if it were food then he will most likely die.

When we say that something has an identity, we are saying that it has a specific nature. A truck, for example, is solid, hard, of a certain mass, and so on; poison has a particular chemical makeup, it acts in a specific manner when it enters the bloodstream, and so on. Living in accordance with the law of identity and the law of noncontradiction is not optional—it is a necessity.

It is not uncommon for philosophers or politicians to come up with an ethical or a political system that does not take into consideration the law of identity. Refusing to accept that a human being is a human being while prescribing codes of behavior for society is like crossing the street while refusing to recognize the nature of a truck—and the consequences are just as serious, only in the case of ethics or politics, on a far greater scale.

While most people find it easy to respect the law of identity when it comes to physical objects like trucks or poison, many of us have a harder time when it comes to our feelings, especially if these feelings are unwanted because they threaten our sense of who we are. If it is important for me to see myself as brave, I may refuse to accept that I sometimes feel fear; if I think of myself as generous, it may be hard for me to accept feelings of envy. But if I am to enjoy psychological health, I need first of all to accept that I feel the way I do. I need to respect reality.

Psychologist Nathaniel Branden regards respect for reality as the foundation of mental health.[4] Self-acceptance—whether accepting the reality of my emotions, my failures, or my successes—is taking the law of identity and applying it to human psychology. In Branden's words, "Self-acceptance is, quite simply, realism. That which is, is. That which I feel, I feel. That which I think, I think. That which I have done, I have done." And just as the law of identity forms the foundation of any coherent and logical philosophy, so is self-acceptance the foundation of a healthy and happy psychology.

TIME-IN Think of experiences that you have had in which you or someone else failed to respect reality and ignored to some extent the law of identity. What was the outcome?

## The Emotion Is the Emotion

In children, violating the law of identity where emotions are concerned can engender perfectionism, and this despite the best-intentioned child-rearing practices. When a parent of a child who is angry says, "You can't be angry over this little thing, can you?" he is challenging the child's actual feeling, encouraging the child to deny the reality of her anger. What the child hears is, "Your anger is not anger." When a child tells her brother, "I hate you," and the parent says, "You don't really hate your brother, you actually love him, don't you?" the parent is negating the existence of an emotion that exists. He is in fact saying, "Your emotion is not really the emotion"—something is not itself.

The most important work on communicating with children was carried out by psychologist Haim Ginott, who, in his book *Between Parent and Child*, writes, "Many people have been educated out of knowing what their feelings are. When they hated, they were told it was only dislike. When they were afraid, they were told there was nothing to be afraid of. When they felt pain, they were advised to be brave and smile."[5] Ginott advocates telling children the truth instead—that hate is hate, that fear is fear, that pain is pain. The parent's role, Ginott says, is to place a mirror to the child's feelings, to teach him about his emotional reality by reflecting his emotions back to him and making them visible, without distortion or analysis: "A child learns about his physical likeness by seeing his image in a mirror. He learns about his emotional likeness by hearing his feelings reflected by us." Just as a mirror does not preach to us but merely shows us what is, a parent should not preach to a child who is in an emotional storm. It is often enough to say, "I see that you are really sad about what just happened" or "It seems to me that you are really feeling angry" to dispel the sadness or anger.

I first read Ginott's book when I was in college and then again when I became a parent and really needed his advice. It never ceases to amaze me how well his approach works, how fast the turnaround can be when the child feels that his feelings are understood. This morning, for instance, David got worked up about the new Superman cap that we bought him yesterday.

"It's too big and I hate it!" he said. "It keeps falling off my head. I hate it!"

I wanted to make him feel better. I also wanted to use the opportunity to teach him that a reaction should be in proportion to the problem. I asked him with empathy, "Aren't you exaggerating a little?"

His response came faster than the speed of Superman. In a loud voice he uttered something that must have been in Kryptonian and started hitting the sofa with the cap. My approach, clearly, was not working.

Fortunately, Ginott, the superpsychologist, came to the rescue, and I changed my tack: "It upsets you, doesn't it, when the cap you like so much doesn't fit you?"

David paused for a moment, looked at me, and said, "Yes."

I continued, "You were so much looking forward to wearing it to day care today, and now it's too big. What a bummer."

"Yes, I really wanted to wear it today."

And then, almost instantaneously, his entire demeanor changed. With a smile on his face, he started walking around the room on his tiptoes. "Daddy, look," he said, "I'm walking like a dinosaur." The crisis was over.

Now, do I think that an ill-fitting Superman hat is a major issue, on a par with, say, the fact that some people do not have enough money for basic clothing? Of course not, and my initial instinct was to make sure David understood that. At the same time, do I think that David's emotions are important, and do I want David to think that his emotions are important? Absolutely, and that is what Ginott reminded me: "When a child is in the midst of strong emotions, he cannot listen to anyone. He cannot accept advice or consolation or constructive criticism. He wants us to understand him." Ginott continues:

> A child's strong feelings do not disappear when he is
> told, "It is not nice to feel that way," or when the parent
> tries to convince him that he "has no reason to feel that

way." Strong feelings do not vanish by being banished; they do diminish in intensity and lose their sharp edges when the listener accepts them with sympathy and understanding. This statement holds true not only for children, but also for adults.

If emotions are running high when we interact with our children, our partners, or anyone else (including ourselves), acknowledging the feelings that are present is often the best thing to do. This can mean holding in check the inclination to help, to preach, to teach, to offer advice. Despite my good intentions, I was heading toward failure by ignoring David's emotions: David would have learned nothing from my sermonizing, and both of us would have been left feeling dissatisfied with our emotional interaction. Instead, Ginott's approach helped me reach a result that benefited everyone: David learned that his emotions matter, I showed him that I understood him, and both of us felt better. And as for the lessons about proportionality and gratitude, I'll find another opportunity to teach him when he is not so worked up.

Clearly, genuine acceptance of our own or others' feelings does not resolve everything. We often need to invest considerable effort and time to work through serious issues. Nonetheless, acceptance is an important first step that has both short-term and long-term implications. In addition to toning down the intensity of the emotion itself, something that, amazingly, can happen almost instantaneously, the long-term effect of reflecting back emotions is that it teaches respect for the law of identity, for reality.

**TIME-IN** Think of times when you or others were in emotional turmoil. Were the emotions acknowledged? Make a mental note to apply the law of identity the next time you or others experience some difficult emotions.

# The Optimal Journey

We are constantly bombarded with perfection. Adonis gracing the cover of *Men's Health* and the flawless Helen on the cover of *Vogue*; women and men on the larger-than-life screen, resolving their conflicts in two hours or less, delivering their perfect lines, making perfect love. We've all heard the self-help gurus tell us that there is no limit to our potential, that what we can believe we can achieve, that where there's a will there's a way. We've been told that we can find perfect bliss if only we follow the road not taken or the road taken by our serene spiritual leader—the one with the best smile on the cover of the *New York Times* bestseller.

But is this picture-perfect ideal that movies, magazines, and books paint for us real? Is the flesh and blood behind the Adonis picture wholly satisfied with his relationships or his investments, and does he not feel threatened by next month's cover boy? Is the non-digitally-enhanced Helen totally happy with her skin or SAT scores, and is she indifferent to the ticking of the clock and the omnipresent force of gravity?

The antidote to perfectionism, and the prescription for optimalism, is acceptance of reality, of what is, be it failures, emotions, or success. When we do not accept failure, we avoid challenge and effort and deprive ourselves of the opportunity to learn and develop; when we do not accept painful emotions, we end up ruminating on them obsessively—we magnify them and deny ourselves the possibility of serenity; and when we fail to accept, embrace, and appreciate success, then nothing we do has real meaning.

Imagine a life of true acceptance. Imagine spending a year in school—reading and writing and learning—without concern for the report card at the end of the ride, accepting success and failure as natural components of development and growth. Imagine being in a relationship without the need to mask imperfections.

Imagine getting up in the morning and accepting the man or woman in the mirror.

Acceptance, however, cannot on its own solve the problem of perfectionism, and expecting it to work miracles will only lead to further unhappiness. I do not believe that there is a quick-fix solution for dealing with perfectionism, or with unhappiness in general. In our search for a happier life through acceptance, we inevitably experience much turmoil. Swayed by promises of heaven on earth, lured by sirens in the odyssey toward self-acceptance, we look for perfect tranquility—and when we do not find it, we feel frustrated and disillusioned. And it is, indeed, an illusion that we can be perfectly accepting and hence perfectly serene. For can anyone living sustain the eternal tranquility of a Mona Lisa?

There is no end point in the journey toward optimalism, no final destination where we have completely accepted ourselves—our failures, our emotions, our successes. The place of eternal bliss and serenity, as far as I can tell, exists only in dreams and magazines. So rather than following Sisyphus's footsteps, why not just drop the burden, let go of the myth of perfection? Why not just be a little easier on ourselves and accept that to fail and succeed is part of a full and fulfilling life, and that to experience fear, jealousy, anger, and, at times, to be *unaccepting* of ourselves is simply, and perfectly, human.

# EXERCISES

## •●● Sentence Completion

Psychologist Nathaniel Branden has developed an exercise called sentence completion, which is about generating a number of endings to an incomplete sentence. The key to doing this exercise is to generate at least six endings to each sentence stem, either aloud or in writing. When doing this exercise, it is important to set aside one's critical faculties and to write or say whatever comes immediately to mind whether or not it makes sense and regardless of internal contradictions and inconsistencies. Sentence completion is itself about the practice of acceptance—expressing whatever comes up, without barriers or inhibitions.

After you complete the exercise, you can go over your responses and identify the ones that make sense to you, the ideas you would like to explore further, and the ones that are irrelevant. You can analyze the endings, write about what you have learned from some of them, and commit to taking action based on your analysis.

Here is an example of a sentence stem that I completed:

If I accept myself 5 percent more . . .
*I will stop working so hard*
*I will not succeed as much*
*I will succeed more*
*I will pursue the things that I love*
*Others will reject me*
*Others will be upset with me*
*I will be more accepting of others*
*Others will be more accepting of me*
*I will no longer need to prove myself constantly*
*I will be calmer*

Here are a few sentence stems for you to try out:

If I give myself the permission to be human . . .
When I reject my emotions . . .
If I become 5 percent less of a Perfectionist . . .
If I become 5 percent more realistic . . .
If I become an Optimalist . . .

> If I appreciate my success 5 percent more . . .
> If I accept failure . . .
> I fear that . . .
> I hope that . . .
> I am beginning to see that . . .

Begin with these stems, and then come up with your own. You can do the sentence-completion exercise every day for a month or once a week; you can complete ten sentences in one sitting or do two stems every day.[6]

## Get Real!

Professor Ellen Langer asked students to assess the intelligence of a number of highly accomplished scientists. The first group of students was given no information on how these scientists attained their success. Participants in this group rated the intelligence of the scientists as extremely high and did not perceive the scientists' achievements as attainable. Participants in the second group were told about the same scientists and the same achievements, but in addition they were told about the trials, errors, and setbacks the scientists experienced on the road to success. Students in this group evaluated these scientists as impressive—just like the students in the first group did. But unlike participants in the first group, students in the second group evaluated the scientists' accomplishments as *attainable*.

The students in the first group were only exposed to the scientists' achievements. They saw only one part of reality—the outcome—which is what a Perfectionist sees. The students in the second group were also aware of what the scientists did along the way. They saw reality as a whole—the process and the outcome—which is what the Optimalist sees.

Needless to say, all achievements come in a series of steps—people study for years, endure many failures, struggle, and experience ups and downs before they "make it." The music world is filled with so-called "overnight successes" who actually worked long and hard before they got their big break. But when we look at the end result, we discount the investment in energy and time that was required to get there, and thus the achievement appears beyond our reach—the work of a superhuman genius. As Langer writes, "By investigating how someone got somewhere, we are more likely to see the achievement as hard-won and our own chances as more plausible. . . . People can imagine themselves taking steps, while great heights seem entirely forbidding."[7]

Write down a goal that you care about, one that you are concerned you may not be able to achieve. In narrative form, describe how you will reach this goal. Include in your story a description of the series of steps that you will take on the road to success, the obstacles and challenges that you will face, and how you will overcome them. Discuss where the pitfalls lie, where you may stumble and fall, and then how you will get up again. Finally, write about how you will eventually get to your destination. Make your story as vivid as possible, narrating it like an adventure story. Repeat this exercise for as many goals as you wish.

Consider that well-researched biographies present the reality of success—these accounts break down achievement to its real components. You may want to read biographies of accomplished individuals, especially those who succeeded in areas that interest you.

# Part 2

# APPLICATIONS

# 5

# Optimal Education

---

**The perfect is the enemy of the good.**

*—Voltaire*

Aristotle, in his discussion of the psychology of the soul, provides a guiding principle that he refers to as the doctrine of the mean, also known as the golden mean. Virtue, according to Aristotle, is not an extreme manifestation of a personal quality but rather lies between insufficiency and excess of that quality. For example, the virtue of courage means behaving neither in a cowardly manner (exhibiting insufficient boldness by fleeing unthinkingly at the slightest sign of danger) nor rashly (exhibiting excessive boldness by plunging headfirst into a dangerous situation without considering potential consequences). Similarly, modesty means finding the happy medium between self-negating humility and arrogance.

Nowhere is finding the right balance between two extremes more important than when it comes to raising and educating children. More than two thousand years after Aristotle, educators and psychologists are showing us how the principle of the golden mean can apply in our homes and in our schools.

# The Underprivileged Privileged

Certain apparent paradoxes that we encounter in students from wealthy families have an important lesson to teach us about education in general. Although these children are materially well off, they are often impoverished in terms of their well-being. Statistically, they have a greater propensity than other children for substance abuse, depression, and anxiety. Psychologist Suniya Luthar and her colleagues have researched the so-called underprivileged privileged, and they have identified two major factors that are responsible for this phenomenon: the pressure to achieve and the feeling of isolation. A related factor, which Luthar discusses indirectly, is the over-involvement by parents and teachers in these children's lives.[1]

Affluent children are often sent to private schools or, in certain neighborhoods, to the best public schools, where the focus is on achieving academic success, taking advanced-level classes, making the honor roll, and entering top colleges. They are under considerable pressure to achieve academically, and in their environment little emphasis is placed on actually enjoying the learning process, on exploring, on learning from failure. The journey is merely a means to an end. Needless to say, the parents' or teachers' intentions are good, but good intentions do not necessarily pave the way to a good place. As Luthar notes, many of us are unaware of the "risks and pressures that can arise, paradoxically, from trying to do the best for our children." For many of these children, these risks and pressures manifest themselves in the form of perfectionism.

Sadly, the system inadvertently reinforces (or at times creates) the obsession with perfection. Who is more likely to be rewarded with an acceptance letter from a top school: a student who explored and got lost, who risked and fell a few times on his way to discovering what he is passionate about, or a student with a flawless transcript? All things being equal, most colleges would admit the latter over the former, rewarding formulaic success rather than courageous failure, measurable results rather than passionate exploration.

Expecting a lot from children is important; one of the common problems in poor neighborhoods is the low expectations that some parents, teachers, and politicians have of children. Demanding standards can potentially lead to healthy, adaptive perfectionism, or what I've been calling optimalism. A child's long-term success and happiness are largely contingent on her pursuing challenging goals while at the same time accepting failure and imperfection. The challenge for parents and educators is to combine high expectations with the permission and encouragement to explore, to take risks, to make mistakes, and to fail.

Of course, it is not only children who are under immense pressure to achieve. Parents, themselves often the product of a similar education, spend most of their waking hours at work, and not necessarily because they wish to. These parents usually have little time or energy left for their children, and the children feel isolated and alone as a result. In the absence of parental presence and support, children are significantly more susceptible to depression and anxiety, as well as to peer pressure. The consequences of parental under-involvement are potentially grave.

And yet the consequences of over-involvement may be just as harmful. When a child feels that whenever her parents are around she is constantly under observation and that every action she takes is being evaluated, when she receives feedback every step of the way and is bombarded with instructions on what she should or shouldn't do, the lesson that she ultimately learns is that there is only one correct way of doing anything—one perfect path that represents the shortest distance between where she is and where she wants to be. No deviations from this path can be tolerated. Over time, the child internalizes the voice that comments on everything she does, and she carries it with her even when her parents are not around.

Parents and teachers often try to accelerate children's development by providing clear directions and by pointing out right from wrong. After all, why shouldn't a parent who is more experienced—who often really does know better—help the child avoid errors that are avoidable? The answer is that although children need and desire guidance, and guidance is good for healthy child development, there can be too much of a good thing. It is equally important to allow children to explore what is for them uncharted territory, to run into dead ends every now and then. Parents with perfectionist tendencies find it especially difficult to let go, to refrain from controlling their child's every move. Such behavior by the parent impedes the child's development. As long as the child is safe, she should be allowed to make her own imperfect decisions, to experience the pain of failing and the pleasure of learning, the pride of success and the vulnerability of independence.

Ironically, excessive parental praise and encouragement may be as detrimental to the child as excessive parental criticism. Some parents, on the advice of psychologists and "parenting experts," provide positive reinforcement every time their child does something right. While positive reinforcement is undoubtedly important, children also need *comment-free periods*—times during which they can engage in work or play that is uninterrupted by either praise or criticism.

Children from affluent families often receive the worst of both worlds. What Luthar and her colleagues found was that the underlying cause of the high levels of substance abuse and distress among teenagers from wealthy backgrounds was typically the "perceived parent criticism for both girls and boys as well as the absence of after-school supervision." On the one hand, parents are insufficiently involved in their children's lives. They spend very little time with them and do not provide adequate after-school supervision. On the other hand, in the limited time that parents do spend with their children, they overcompensate for their overall absence and become excessively involved, which leads to "perceived parent criticism."

Research on first-born children provides additional insight into the delicate balance, the golden mean, between over-involvement and under-involvement.[2] An eldest child is more likely to be classified as gifted, and a disproportionate number of students in top colleges are first-born. This is due, at least in part, to the extra time and attention these children receive from their parents. However, at the same time, the eldest child is also more likely than his siblings to become a Perfectionist. This, too, is partially due to the fact that his parents have more time to spend with him, which also means that he is supervised more closely and enjoys fewer comment-free periods. While some parents feel guilty for not being as attentive to their second or third child as they were to their first, they may actually be doing their younger children a favor. Having said that, the need to provide children the space to meander is not a license for negligence: there are clear and indisputable benefits to parental involvement. To paraphrase Aristotle, writing about the doctrine of the mean, the key is to be involved at the right time, to the right degree, with the right motive, and in the right way. Of course, as any parent knows, this is easier said than done.

A prime example of the educational golden mean in action can be found in Montessori schools. The aim of the Montessori classroom is to create "freedom in a structured environment." Freedom without structure or boundaries is under-involvement; structure or boundaries without freedom is over-involvement.[3] It is hard not to be impressed by the calm intensity of Montessori schoolchildren who are utterly absorbed in their individual or group tasks. While the child knows that the teacher is there for her if she needs help, and while the teacher praises as well as criticizes when appropriate, the actual involvement of the teacher is reduced to the bare minimum: as much involvement as necessary and as little involvement as possible. The teacher is in effect creating a safe environment, one that is appropriate for the child's age. The child is then allowed to act independently within that environment, whether by putting a set of objects through a hole or exploring a big question about the origin of our species.

Mihaly Csikszentmihalyi, who was seminal in launching the positive psychology movement, has conducted research with Kevin Rathunde comparing Montessori schools to traditional ones.[4] One of the major differences was that in traditional schools, students spend much of their time listening to lectures and taking notes, which is a highly structured activity. By contrast, in Montessori schools, students spend more time involved in independent projects, whether individually or in groups. This type of activity provides a combination of freedom and structure. Not coincidentally, Montessori students had more favorable perceptions of their fellow students, their teachers, and their school. They were more engaged in their schoolwork and more energetic and reported higher levels of intrinsic motivation.

**TIME-IN** Do you create for others, whether children or adults, an environment conducive to learning, with sufficient comment-free periods and adequate involvement? Do you enjoy such an environment in your own life?

# The Good-Enough Parent

Work on child development by influential British pediatrician and psychoanalyst Donald Winnicott sheds light on healthy parental involvement.[5] While Winnicott focuses on the role of the mother, his ideas apply as much to the father and indeed to anyone who is actively and directly involved in child rearing.

Initially, says Winnicott, the child is completely dependent on the mother: there is full physical and psychological symbiosis. What the child needs at this stage is for the mother to respond to his every wish, whether it is to be fed or to be held. Gradually, to help the child mature through the process of differentiation—becoming an independent, fully functioning individual—the mother has to pull back. Rather than responding perfectly—in other words, immediately and fully—to her child's every need, Winnicott says, she should respond adequately. This imperfect caretaker, who Winnicott calls the good-enough mother, "starts off with an almost complete adaptation to her infant's needs, and as time proceeds she adapts less and less completely, gradually, according to the infant's growing ability to deal with her failure."

The good-enough mother does not abandon the child, but she does allow him to struggle. For example, rather than immediately responding to his need to be coddled each time he cries, the mother slowly, over time, lets the child experience some discomfort on his own—as long as he is safe, of course. When the child learns that he cannot always rely on his mother, he learns to rely on—and soothe—himself. As the mother gradually and sensitively "fails" the child with increasing frequency—as she engages in what Winnicott describes as "graduated failure of adaptation"—the child develops the ability to deal with the external world independent of her. Given that failure is an inevitable part of the real world, the mother who truly cares about her child prepares him by simulating, in a controlled environment and at a pace that is suitable for the child, what he will eventually have to deal with by himself.

The process of separation—the time lags during which the crying child, for instance, confronts the mother's absence—is unpleasant, to say the least, and difficult for both parent and child. There is, however, no way around it. A child would never learn to walk if he were perfectly protected—if he were constantly held up, supported, deprived of the unpleasant experience of falling down. We either learn to fail or we fail to learn.

We can extend this idea of the good-enough mother—or, more generally, the good-enough parent—to apply also to the infant's behavior, not just to his needs. For example, a perfect parent would be reluctant to let the infant make a mess while eating; she would either feed the child herself or constantly hover around him, cleaning up after him every time he spills something. A good-enough parent recognizes the importance of learning by doing, of getting one's hands dirty, and will allow the baby to drop some food, smear his face, bring empty spoons to his mouth, and stick food in his hair. At the same time, the good-enough parent makes sure that the baby gets enough food and is not in danger of poking himself with a fork. Finding the right amount of involvement, the parent allows room for failure while not compromising on the child's health and safety.

Good-enough parenting is important for healthy development throughout infancy, childhood, and adolescence. For instance, in contrast to the good-enough parent who is able to find the golden mean between negligence and overindulgence, the "perfect" parent continuously caters to all his teenager's material and psychological needs. The child is showered with gifts; whatever she wants she has only to ask for—assuming, that is, she hasn't already been provided with the financial means to buy these things for herself. But there is another kind of indulgence that is even more damaging, and that is the emotional and intellectual sanitizing of the child's environment: if a teacher or a classmate is disagreeable to the child, if the child struggles with a certain subject or project, the parent (or the parent's representative) solves the problem. While part of a parent's role is to help the child when necessary, solving, or trying to solve, every problem for the child, in every possible situation, can do more harm than good.

Many parents who have experienced personal hardship desire a better life for their children. To want to spare your children from having to go through unpleasant experiences is a noble aim, and it naturally stems from love and concern for the child. What these parents don't realize, however, is that while in the short term they may be making the lives of their children more pleasant, in the long term they may be preventing their children from acquiring self-confidence, resilience, a sense of meaning, and important interpersonal skills. As Samuel Smiles, a nineteenth-century English author, wrote, "It is doubtful whether any heavier curse could be imposed on man than the complete gratification of all his wishes without effort on his part, leaving nothing for his hopes, desires or struggles."[6] For healthy development, to grow and mature, the child needs to deal with some failure, struggle through some difficult periods, and experience some painful emotions. As a parent, I often wish there were shortcuts, or ways around the hardship, but there aren't any.

TIME-IN Reflect on your relationship with a child—your own or someone else's—and think of opportunities to be "good enough," finding the golden mean between under-involvement and over-involvement.

Our schools are full of Perfectionists. Short of turning back the clock and engaging in different child rearing or early education practices, what can teachers or parents do about a perfectionist child? And if the child is not a Perfectionist, how can the educator ensure that she remains that way? Understanding Carol Dweck's research on fixed mind-set and growth mind-set and the distinction between person and behavior can help educators inoculate the child against the bug of perfectionism.

## Mind-Set

Dweck distinguishes between a fixed mind-set and a growth mind-set.[7] A fixed mind-set is the belief that our abilities—our intelligence, physical competence, personality, and interpersonal skills—are essentially set in stone and cannot really change. We are either gifted and talented, in which case we'll succeed in school, at work, in sports, and in our relationships, or we are permanently deficient and consequently doomed to failure. In contrast, a growth mind-set is the belief that our abilities are malleable—that they can, and do, change throughout our lives; we are born with certain abilities, but these provide a mere starting point, and to succeed we have to apply ourselves, dedicate time, invest a great deal of effort.

For a person with a fixed mind-set, hard work is threatening, as it indicates that her abilities are limited and that, by extension, she is, too. After all, if she were gifted and talented, then she wouldn't need to work. Not wanting to appear deficient, and given her belief that nothing can be done to remedy a deficiency, she constantly feels the pressure to prove to herself and to others how smart, competent, and perfect she already is.

The experience of a person with a growth mind-set is radically different. For her, hard work is not only necessary, it is also fun and exciting; she enjoys the journey because, rather than trying to prove herself constantly, her primary focus is learning, developing, and realizing her potential. In addition to being happier, a person with a growth mind-set is more persistent in her efforts and is therefore more likely to succeed. There are, of course, people with a fixed mind-set who work hard, but they are usually driven by the need to prove to themselves and to others how smart they are. It is a heavy burden to carry.

Thankfully, the fixed mind-set itself is not fixed! In a seminal study, Dweck and her colleagues randomly assigned fifth-grade students to two groups. In the first round of the study, students in both groups were given ten fairly difficult questions; they generally did well on the test and answered most of the questions correctly. After completing the task, participants in both groups were praised but in different ways. In the first group, the fixed mind-set was induced by praising participants for their intelligence (along the lines of "you must be smart at this"), while the growth mind-set was induced in the second group by praising participants for their efforts (along the lines of "you must have worked really hard").

In the second round of the study, participants had to choose between taking a new test that was difficult and from which they would learn and taking one that was easy and quite similar to the one they had just taken. Ninety percent of the students in the group in which the growth mind-set was induced, who had been praised for their efforts, chose the difficult test that offered them an opportunity to learn. By contrast, most of the students in the fixed mind-set group, who had been praised for their intelligence, opted for the familiar over the challenging and chose to take the easier test.

In the third round of the study, students from both groups were given a test that was too hard for them to solve. Those previously praised for their intelligence were miserable as they struggled, while those praised for their effort actually enjoyed themselves— the struggling and the learning. As Dweck explains, "Emphasizing effort gives a child a variable that they can control. They come to see themselves as in control of their success. Emphasizing natural intelligence takes it out of the child's control, and it provides no good recipe for responding to a failure."

Interestingly, when Dweck then gave both groups one final test with the same difficulty level as the very first test they took, the "smart" students performed about 20 percent worse than they had in the first round of the study. By contrast, the "hardworking" students performed 30 percent better than they had before. As this study demonstrates, the growth mind-set leads to taking on new challenges, to greater enjoyment when facing challenges, and, finally, to better performance overall.

Dweck was able to induce fixed or growth mind-sets with a single sentence, by praising either the students' intelligence or their effort. Her findings are both disturbing (because they show how much impact ordinary words that we utter can have on our children) and encouraging (because we know how we can easily make a significant and positive impact). We need to praise children for their efforts, for that which is under their control, rather than for their intelligence, which is not. In her book *Mind-set*, Dweck writes:

> Parents think they can hand children permanent confidence—like a gift—by praising their brains and talent. It doesn't work, and in fact has the opposite effect. It makes children doubt themselves as soon as anything is hard or anything goes wrong. If parents want to give

their children a gift, the best thing they can do is to teach their children to love challenges, be intrigued by mistakes, enjoy effort, and keep on learning.

The fixed mind-set is akin to perfectionism, the growth mind-set to optimalism. Praising intelligence induces the fear of failure, because it engenders the belief that being truly intelligent ought to preclude the possibility of failure. In contrast, praising effort shifts the focus to the journey and away from outcome; whether one succeeds or fails matters less than whether or not one works hard. A fixed mind-set (the Perfectionist) leads to an intense fear of failure and to catastrophizing failure when it does happen; a growth mind-set (the Optimalist) leads to perceiving failure as an opportunity for growth and development.

Educators should constantly emphasize the process—the hard work, the effort, the enjoyment of the journey, the importance of failures as learning opportunities—rather than the raw achievement and the outcome. Telling children how smart they are leads to a short-term high (for the child, as well as for the parent or teacher!), while in the long term it hurts the child's motivation, performance, and well-being. Parents and teachers should constantly be asking children what they learned—from others, from books, from their own mistakes and successes—and in what ways they have improved, not what prizes and grades they received and what the competition was like.

Children also have to understand that they don't have to be the best at everything and that just having fun is a legitimate reason for doing something. At the same time, if they do want to excel, then effort is necessary—which does not preclude the possibility of having fun along the way.

Whenever I fall into the perfectionist trap and experience an intense and debilitating fear of failure, I remind myself that ability is malleable, that ups and downs are natural, and that with effort I can improve, as I have often done in the past. The growth mind-set focuses me on the journey, and the pressure subsides. I do it for myself—to enhance my performance and enjoyment—and I do it for my children and students who are more likely to do what I do rather than what I say.

**TIME-IN** Think about an ability or a skill that you have improved over time as a result of your efforts. It could be anything from your ability on the tennis court to your speaking skills, from your courage to your empathy. What did you do to improve this ability or skill?

It is important to point out that Dweck's distinction between the fixed and the growth mind-sets is different from Sowell's distinction between the constrained and the unconstrained views of human nature. Dweck looks at our abilities while Sowell looks at our nature. The Optimalist generally subscribes to the constrained view of human nature (the belief that our nature is fixed) and at the same time espouses the growth mind-set (the belief that our abilities are not fixed). The Perfectionist generally believes the opposite to be true—that our nature is not fixed (unconstrained view) and that our abilities are fixed (fixed mind-set).

## Tradition and Progress

When I was in Australia last year, I happened to listen to a radio program in which a group of business leaders were complaining about the most recent crop of university graduates. These smart, well-educated twenty-somethings entering the workforce needed endless pampering and praise, and when criticized they would often sulk or even quit their jobs. Managers in the United States and throughout the Western world are facing the same problem. To the older generation, many of whom were educated in the school of hard knocks, the phenomenon of the spoiled and weak newcomer spells trouble.

Carol Dweck calls these newcomers "the praised generation." They are often the product of well-meaning parents and teachers who, out of a desire to raise the children's self-esteem, tended to offer constant and unconditional praise (to strengthen the ego) while refraining from any form of criticism (which might damage the fragile ego). The results, however, were often the opposite of those intended: instead of becoming adults with high self-esteem, the children turned out to be insecure and spoiled. According to Dweck, "We now have a workforce full of people who need constant reassurance and can't take criticism. Not a recipe for success in business, where taking on challenges, showing persistence, and admitting and correcting mistakes are essential."

The future, it seems, does not hold greater promise. A new generation of children is being raised by adults who applaud loudly and reprimand meekly. One reason for doing so is the natural desire of parents and educators to be liked and the assumption that the child will like them more if they are generous with praise and frugal with criticism. In fact, however, children know (though not always immediately) that they need boundaries, and therefore educators are more likely in the long term to be appreciated for being real, for calling it as they see it—the good with the bad, the praise with the criticism. A forthright parent who sets clear boundaries is more likely to earn respect over time than a parent who aspires to be liked and consequently caters unreflectively to the child's whims.

But it's not just the need to be liked that drives educators. Modern educational practices, it should be remembered, developed in reaction to a long history of harsh and often cruel teaching methods, in which parents and teachers ruled with an iron hand. Those who suffered under such practices understandably wanted to replace the stick with a carrot. With the publication of his book *Democracy and Education* in 1916, John Dewey, considered by many to be the father of modern American education, launched the progressive education movement.[8] The child, no longer devoid of rights, was placed on an equal footing with the educator. Rather than commanding the child, the educator was to ask the child; rather than bending or, if necessary, breaking the child's spirit, the educator was to nurture and support the child.

This was an important change in the history of education, but as is often the case with a movement born in reaction to something else, the change went too far to the other extreme. The laissez-faire progressive schools in which criticism was scarce and praise plentiful did not produce well-rounded, self-confident, highly educated children but rather restless and insecure graduates. Dewey was not blind to the potentially negative effects of progressive education. He realized that he—or those who interpreted and implemented his theory—had gone too far. He wrote another book, *Experience and Education*, calling for a more nuanced synthesis between the old and the new, but unfortunately this book received little attention.[9] For half a century the effects of progressive education were not as grave as they might have been. The external reality that the students faced—the Great Depression followed by World War II—made tough men and women out of the soft boys and girls.

Then came the Sixties. A generation of rebels wanted to break the shackles of traditional education. They applied their new sense of freedom to the raising of their children. But in their eagerness to do away with the harshness of traditional educational methods, they also dispensed with discipline and boundaries. Their children, born in the sixties, seventies, and eighties, did not by and large have the "benefit" of the hardships that previous generations had been exposed to; there was nothing there to toughen them and prepare them for life's challenges. The overpraised generation remained spoiled.

Ironically, despite being polar opposites, the two approaches to education—the traditional and the progressive—result in similar perfectionist tendencies. A child educated in the traditional way is punished for every deviation from the narrow, straight path. His education does not prepare him to look at failures as learning opportunities, and he learns to fear failure. The person educated in the progressive mold does not learn how to fail and rebound from failure, and therefore he, too, learns to fear it. After all, nothing he has done was subject to criticism or punishment; sooner or later, when no longer protected by his teachers or parents, he faces the real-world consequences of failure. Unprepared, he is lost and afraid.

So what can be done? The solution is to find the golden mean between the old methods and the new. In this case, the key is learning to separate the person from the behavior.

## Person and Behavior

When we, as teachers and parents, focus on our students' and children's inherent worth, we are able to bring out the best in them. We must learn to appreciate the child as a person—to see her essence beyond SAT scores, school grades, success and failure. We need to create an environment in which children can develop a sense of self-worth that is not dependent on standardized tests or the images that they see reflected in society's mirror. In the words of Carl Rogers, children, as much as possible, have to feel "unconditional positive regard" from their parents and teachers.

All this is the part of the equation that progressive education largely got right. The other part, which progressive education largely missed, is the need to set very clear boundaries on behavior. "Unconditional positive regard" is not synonymous with "anything goes." A child who brings home a poor report card because she slacked off can and should be reprimanded. A child who purposely and unjustly hurts another child deserves punishment. So while children need to feel that they themselves are unconditionally accepted by the significant adults in their lives, they also have to know that there are behaviors that the adults will not accept. Marva Collins, an extraordinary schoolteacher who has transformed the lives of thousands of students, gives teachers this advice:

> When you must reprimand your child, do so in a loving manner. Don't ever try to degrade or humiliate him. His ego is a precious thing worth preserving. Try saying:
>
> "I love you very much but I will not have this kind of behavior."
>
> "Do you know why I won't tolerate that? Simply because you are too bright to behave that way."[10]

Focusing on behavior, the parent can say, "You played when you should have studied, and you put very little effort into your schoolwork. Next time, I expect you to work harder so that you can do better." If the child does not respond to verbal criticism, she can be punished by being grounded or by being deprived of a game that she likes.

Separating the person from the behavior is equally important when dealing with success. Parents are often quick to praise the child and convey to him how much they love him (explicitly or implicitly) when he performs well. And when the child feels that Mom and Dad love him more if he does well, he extrapolates that they will love him less if he does less well. The child begins to fear failure because he understands that his parents' love is conditional. As Ginott points out, praise should deal "only with the child's efforts and accomplishments, *not* with his character and personality."

Telling a child that she is wonderful for earning a good report card or terrible when she brings home a poor report card focuses on her person; telling the child that she has worked hard or that she did not work hard enough focuses on her behavior. That the child is wonderful in her parents' eyes must be a given—whether performance is good or bad. Parents and educators who praise or criticize the person are increasing the likelihood of perfectionism in the child; focusing on the behavior, both in praise and in criticism, is more likely to lead to optimalism.

**TIME-IN** How do you praise children and adults? Do you focus on effort and process? Make a mental note to do so in the future.

As teachers and parents, we can go a long way toward correcting the obsession in our culture with praising external success. Because so much in our world conspires to glorify measurable success, a child very early on internalizes the idea that to be valued he needs to bring home a good evaluation and that net worth is a prerequisite for self-worth. Parents and teachers can create an alternative environment in which love and support are there throughout the journey and not just when the child reaches the destination.

# EXERCISE

## My Best Teacher

Write about the best teacher you've ever had. It could be your parent, a first-grade teacher, a college professor, or a boss who invested a great deal in your professional development. What was it about this teacher that brought out the best in you? What can you learn from this teacher when it comes to dealing with children?

Now think about how you function as a teacher in various areas in your life. How can you apply the lessons you learned from your teacher in the workplace, at home, and in other areas of your life? You can repeat the exercise, this time reflecting on another teacher and comparing him or her to the first one. What are some of the similarities and differences between the two? What else can you learn about effective teaching that you can apply to your role as a teacher?

# 6

# Optimal Work

If you want to increase your success rate, double
your failure rate.

*—Thomas J. Watson*

A my Edmondson, a professor at Harvard Business School,
was a doctoral student when I was an undergraduate. We
both worked with Professor Richard Hackman, one of
the leading scholars in the field of organizational behavior. In
her research, Amy wanted to show that hospital staff who were
members of groups that met Hackman's conditions for effective
teamwork—conditions such as clear and compelling goals and
appropriate resources—were less likely to make medical errors.

This was obviously important research, as patients are occasionally injured and sometimes even die as a result of avoidable errors.
Moreover, there is a high financial cost to medical mistakes, not
least because of malpractice lawsuits and insurance costs. After
years of data collection, data entry, and calculations, Amy had her
results, and, as she had hoped, they were statistically significant—
but not in the way she had expected. Groups that met Hackman's conditions for effectiveness seemed to make *more* mistakes

rather than fewer. This contradicted decades of research. What was going on? How could well-led teams be making *more* errors? And then it dawned on her that the good teams "don't make more mistakes, they report more."[1]

Amy went back to the hospital to test her revised hypothesis, and what she found was indeed that the teams that met Hackman's conditions for success were making significantly fewer errors. Because members of the teams that did not meet these conditions were concealing their errors, to the outside observer it seemed that they were making fewer errors, when in fact they were making more. It was only with respect to errors that could not be concealed—such as the death of a patient—that it was clear which groups were getting it wrong more often.

Amy's research took the concept of "learn to fail or fail to learn" from the individual realm and applied it to groups and organizations.[2] In a world where change is the only constant, where personal improvement and organizational learning are essential for competitiveness, fear of reporting a failure is a recipe for long-term failure. Well-led teams, Amy discovered, enjoyed *psychological safety*—the confidence that no member of the team would be embarrassed or punished if she spoke out, asked for assistance, or failed in a specific task.[3] When team leaders create a climate of psychological safety, when members feel comfortable "failing" and then sharing and discussing their mistakes, all members of the team can learn and improve. In contrast, when mistakes are concealed, learning is less likely to take place, and the likelihood that errors will be repeated is higher.

In the 1980s the Israeli Air Force instituted a no-blame policy that encouraged pilots and units to report errors and near misses. The removal of the threat of punishment created a safe organizational environment within which learning could take place. The effect of the policy was that the number of reported errors increased, while the number of actual errors decreased significantly. The U.S. Air Force has a similar policy in place: pilots are not penalized for errors, provided they report them within twenty-four hours. However, pilots who attempt to conceal errors and are found out are punished.

## Learning from Failure

By creating a psychologically safe environment, great corporate leaders increase the likelihood of bringing out the Optimalist in every employee. Robert Wood Johnson II (also known as General Johnson) took a small family business and transformed it into one of the largest pharmaceutical and medical device manufacturers in the world. Johnson & Johnson has been extremely successful, not least because its management understands the importance of learning from mistakes.

Early on in his career, Jim Burke, the highly successful CEO of Johnson & Johnson for thirteen years until his retirement in 1989, was taught by General Johnson the importance of learning from mistakes. After Burke developed a new product that turned out to be a total dud, he was called in by General Johnson, who was chairman of the board at the time. Burke expected to be fired. Instead, General Johnson extended his hand and said:

> I just want to congratulate you. All business is making decisions, and if you don't make decisions you won't have any failures. The hardest job I have is getting people to make decisions. If you make the same decision wrong again, I'll fire you. But I hope you'll make a lot of others, and that you'll understand there are going to be more failures than successes.

Burke went on to embrace the same philosophy when he became CEO: "We don't grow unless we take risks. Any successful company is riddled with failures." Before joining Johnson & Johnson, Burke had failed at three other businesses. By making his failures public, by telling and retelling the story of his encounter with General Johnson, Burke sent an important message to his employees.

**TIME-IN** Think about an error that was made at an organization you worked for or that you know well. What was learned from the mistake? What more could have been learned?

Great managers become great by allowing themselves and others to fail and to learn from mistakes. Typically, however, when we read about these corporate leaders, we are told a lot about their achievements and very little (if anything) about the many mistakes that paved the road to success. Just as very few people know about Babe Ruth's strikeout record or the number of times Michael Jordan missed a game-winning shot, few people know about the numerous failures experienced by the innovative founder of Virgin Group Richard Branson, or the courageous Washington Post CEO Katharine Graham, or the resourceful Time Warner chairman Richard Parsons, or the legendary president of IBM Thomas Watson.

Many leaders or aspiring leaders erroneously believe that their role models' road to success was free of failures or mistakes. Trying to emulate their heroes, they themselves do all that they can to avoid or hide failure. They stop taking risks (failing to learn from failure) and become extremely defensive (failing to learn from feedback). Maintaining the appearance of perfection becomes more important than learning and growing. Sidney Finkelstein, who studied major business mistakes in more than fifty organizations, notes:

> Ironically enough, the higher people are in the management hierarchy, the more they tend to supplement their perfectionism with blanket excuses, with CEOs usually being the worst of all. For example, in one organization we studied, the CEO spent the entire forty-five-minute interview explaining all the reasons why others were to blame for the calamity that hit his company. Regulators, customers, the government, and even other executives within the firm—all were responsible. No mention was made, however, of personal culpability.[4]

This attitude among business leaders is harmful. First, employees follow the example of their boss, doing what he does rather than what he says. If a manager never admits to failure or never learns from his mistakes, then his calls to his employees to do so will likely fall on deaf ears. Second, such behavior only exacerbates what Daniel Goleman calls the CEO disease—"the information vacuum around a leader created when people withhold important (and usually unpleasant) information."[5]

The CEO disease is common in organizations. Management consultant Tom Peters points out that "senior managers will be shielded from most bad news," particularly when employees notice that their boss receives bad news with resistance, with excuses, or, worst, by shooting the messenger.

The reluctance of subordinates to provide feedback deprives leaders of one of the most important developmental resources available to them. Traditionally, the boss commented on the performance of his employees; to this day managers tend to feel more comfortable when feedback, especially negative feedback, flows from the top down rather than in the other direction. As it turns out, however, the appraisal by employees of their boss tends to be more accurate and a better predictor of long-term success than the appraisal by the boss of her subordinates.[6] As Jack Welch, Bill George, Anita Roddick, and other successful leaders have often stated, facing reality is one of the pillars of successful individuals and successful companies. When accurate information that is in the possession of employees does not reach the higher echelons, management loses out, as does the organization as a whole.

If a manager's behavior toward employees is harsh and disrespectful, employees will naturally feel reluctant to speak up. However, being pleasant and respectful is not always enough. To inoculate the organization against the CEO disease, the leader must consistently solicit feedback, generously reward honesty, and make sure that the bearer of bad news will be treated at least as well as the bearer of good news. Leaders, whether in business or elsewhere, must create an environment in which people not only are permitted to deliver the news that no one wants to hear but are actively encouraged to do so.

**TIME-IN** Do you know a leader who creates an environment that is conducive to learning from mistakes? What are some of the specific things that this leader does?

Learning from failure is easier said than done. In their work on organizational learning, Mark Cannon and Amy Edmondson show that while most organizations pay lip service to the importance of learning from mistakes, very few organizations actually do so in practice.[7] This is because *looking* good is often a stronger motivation than *being* good (by owning up to, and learning from, one's failures). Cannon and Edmondson suggest dealing with the pervasive fear of failure by reframing our view of mistakes:

"As human beings, we are socialized to distance ourselves from failures. Reframing failure so that we regard it not as something associated with shame and weakness but as something associated with risk, uncertainty and improvement is a critical first step on the learning journey." The leader who is able to change the way members of her organization perceive failure is well on her way to creating a true learning organization, one that is competitive, adaptive, resilient, and pleasant to work for.

## Perfectionism and Micromanagement

In some of the most insightful work done on perfectionism and workplace performance, Robert Hurley and James Ryman distinguish between apprehensive Perfectionists and healthy Perfectionists.[8] The apprehensive Perfectionist is primarily driven by the fear of making mistakes or failing to meet his own (or others') expectations of him. His primary motivation is avoiding failure, and he "plays not to lose." The healthy Perfectionist, what I call the Optimalist, does not like failing either, but he recognizes that, like everyone else, he is fallible and that failure provides an opportunity for learning. His primary motivation is achieving excellence, and he "plays to win."

The performance and job satisfaction of the apprehensive Perfectionist suffer, as do those of his employees. The most common behavior that the apprehensive Perfectionist displays is micromanagement, which is his attempt to eliminate the possibility of mistakes among his subordinates.

Obviously, there are times when closely scrutinizing employees' work is exactly what a manager should be doing. For example, preparing a comprehensive report to potential investors that could determine the future of the organization is important, and the manager in charge should check and recheck for errors among those contributing to the report. But when, regardless of the importance of the project, the manager scrutinizes every action taken by every employee under the guise of "making sure" or "responsible practice," then there is a problem.

To know when to wield control and when to yield it is the mark of an optimalist manager. While there is, unfortunately, no precise formula, a useful principle to follow is to exercise as much control as necessary and as little control as possible. Contrary to the Perfectionist's belief, not all failures are created equal. In situations where the consequences of imperfect performance are relatively harmless, it is best to relax managerial control as far as possible. This provides a great opportunity for subordinates to undertake independent work and gives them the chance to take real risks. If the subordinates succeed, they grow as they develop confidence. If they fail, they grow as they learn without the organization having incurred too much harm in the process. Moreover, subordinates, especially competent ones, are likely to leave a workplace if they feel that they are unnecessarily micromanaged. The perfectionist manager loses out, as do his employees and the organization: the best people leave, and those who remain fail to learn.

## Working Hard, Working Smart

One of the consequences of unhealthy perfectionism that Hurley and Ryman point to is burnout, a phenomenon familiar to many Perfectionists, myself included. As far back as I can remember, I knew that hard work is the key to success. The two quotes that are etched in my mind are "There is no substitute for hard work" (attributed to Thomas Edison) and "The harder I work, the luckier I get" (attributed to Thomas Jefferson). When I played squash, competitors would sometimes say behind my back that if they had trained as hard as I had, they also could have won the championship. For me, this was the greatest compliment (even if usually not intended as such), because they were probably right.

The Perfectionist in me, though, at times took the mantra of hard work too far, or rather in the wrong direction. For many years I was emotionally sustained by another quote, made famous by California's governor when he was still the Terminator: "I am a machine." As a sportsman, I was flattered when squash aficionados noted that I trained and played like a well-oiled machine; my approach to the game was scientific and systematic, I was hardworking and disciplined, I rarely showed emotion on court, and no matter how tired I was, I never allowed my opponent to know it. This approach usually served me well, but it also exacted a high price when I applied it indiscriminately. Consistency and endurance are important to success. But to aspire to machinelike qualities where emotions are concerned—to ignore one's feelings and needs—is a prescription for unhappiness and, ultimately, failure. The constant stress that I experienced while playing squash, the burnout in the form of lost motivation and waning drive, the injuries that eventually ended my career—all of these were products of the perfectionist, machinelike approach.

In the 1960s Australian Derek Clayton was among the least gifted marathon runners in the world. Six feet two inches tall with a relatively low oxygen-intake capacity, he had a body type that was anything but ideal for long-distance running. Nevertheless, he made up for his imperfect physical attributes by working harder than anyone else, running as many as 160 miles a week. While his grueling regime initially paid off, he eventually hit a brick wall, reaching what appeared to be the limit of his natural potential. With a personal best of over two hours and seventeen minutes, more than five minutes slower than the world's best time, he could not quite compete with the top runners of his generation. Beyond a certain point, working harder, piling on the miles, did not lead to improved performance.

But it did lead to injuries. Preparing for the 1967 Fukuoka marathon in Japan, Clayton was forced to take an entire month off to recuperate from his injuries. Disappointed that his momentum was disrupted by injury, he nevertheless decided to run the Japanese marathon as part of his preparation for the subsequent race. To his and everyone else's surprise, after an entire month with no training, Clayton proceeded to break his personal record by more than eight minutes, becoming the first person in history to run a marathon in under two hours and ten minutes. In 1969 he was injured again, this time while preparing for the Antwerp marathon. Following his forced period of inactivity, Clayton again broke his personal and world record, stopping the clock at two hours, eight minutes, thirty-three seconds. This record held for twelve years.

Clayton's story and others like it highlight the importance of recovery. Today, one would be hard pressed to find a coach or an athlete who does not take the need for rest as seriously as he does the need for intensive training. Sadly, this understanding has not caught on in the workplace. Driven employees settle for nothing less than hard work followed by even harder work. Demanding managers expect machinelike performance from their teams and think nothing of expecting their employees to be available by e-mail or by phone on weekends and on vacation. Moreover, employees often internalize their managers' expectations; they feel guilty if they are not in the office on the weekend, and they interrupt their own vacation to monitor e-mails obsessively and to make sure that everything is running smoothly in their absence.

In their work on "corporate athletes," Jim Loehr and Tony Schwartz demonstrate that to achieve peak performance on the field or in the office we must take into consideration our human needs—specifically, the need for recovery.⁹ Failure to do so exacts a high price from individual employees, as well as from the organization as a whole. As Loehr and Schwartz note, "Executives need to learn what world-class athletes already know: recovering energy is as important as expending it."

## Recovery

Clayton was a Perfectionist, believing that the harder he worked, the better he would become. Then physical injuries forced him against his will to behave like an Optimalist. Reluctantly, he took time off for recovery—and realized his potential. In the psychological realm, injuries come in the form of emotional harm; feeling lethargic, anxious, or depressed are some of the signals that we need some time to recover. These signals, unlike physical injuries, are more subtle and easier to discount. And it is not uncommon for a person to continue working just as hard, if not harder, while the mind and the heart are pleading for a break.

Emotional signals can be ignored or suppressed with drugs. Taking in some caffeine for a 3 p.m. energy boost may be fine (assuming an afternoon nap is not an option), but regularly relying on caffeine to stay awake because we only get three or four hours of sleep is physically and psychologically unhealthy. Similarly, addiction to nicotine, alcohol, or other relaxants is not a substitute for taking time to relax in a natural way, by breathing deeply or exercising. Psychiatric medication is necessary in some situations but not when the painful emotions are simply a result of working ourselves into depression. Painful emotions are the body's natural warning system, and we disregard them at our peril.

Inadequate rest is, of course, not the only cause of lethargy, anxiety, or depression, but in the kind of world we live in, it is a major cause. There is nothing wrong with hard work per se. Long hours and a focused effort can be beneficial, as long as the time you spend at the office does not come at the expense of other activities that could make you happier. The problem in today's corporate world, as well as in many other realms, is not hard work; the problem is insufficient recovery.

## Multilevel Recovery

A robot will not get anxious or depressed, tired or injured; it may perhaps require some fine-tuning once in a while, a new battery, or a spare part but otherwise does not need much by way of maintenance. But imagine a robot—or a computer, a car, or a TV set, for that matter—that needs to shut down for fifteen minutes every couple of hours, that needs to spend eight hours of every twenty-four-hour cycle turned off, that needs to recharge for a full day after every five or six full-day cycles. Oh, and to top it all, the robot needs two to four weeks' downtime each year. A lousy machine. And a real, fully functioning human being.

According to Loehr and Schwartz, we need to replace the metaphor we currently use to describe the way we work. We should not think of the employee as a marathon runner who works long and hard until she drops but as a sprinter who alternates intensive work and recovery. This new metaphor should be applied to the micro-, mid-, and macrolevels of recovery.

On the microlevel, rather than trying to push ourselves for fourteen hours with little rest (the marathon runner mode), we need to alternate between work and rest: ninety minutes or so of intensive work followed by at least fifteen minutes of full recovery.

Recovery can come in the form of meditating, exercising, listening to music, spending time with family or friends, having a quiet meal, taking a walk around the block, chatting with coworkers, or doing anything else we enjoy and find relaxing. Whether our workday is six or sixteen hours long, we need to punctuate it with regular breaks.

Most people, if they are not too tired, can maintain focused intensity at work for anywhere between one and two hours at a time. After that, performance drops and we get significantly less return for our effort. Taking a short break helps recharge our energy levels, and we are again able to sustain focused intensity. Needless to say, the cycle of ninety minutes on and fifteen minutes off cannot go on indefinitely, and after a while we need a longer break.

Midlevel recovery includes adequate sleep, which for most people means between seven and nine hours in each twenty-four-hour period. If we deprive ourselves of sleep on a regular basis and rely instead on chemical stimulants to keep us awake, we pay a price in the form of decreased creativity and productivity, as well as an increased risk of depression and anxiety. A day of rest each week is critical for recovery. Even God needed a day off! In fact, people who put their work aside for a day each week report that they are more creative and productive the rest of the week.

Recovery on the macrolevel is about taking a vacation—a week to a month off at least once a year. While many Type A individuals feel guilty taking time off, they should keep in mind that relaxing for a while is a good investment. We get our best ideas and are most creative when we introduce space into our tight schedules: the connection between recreation and creation is not just etymological. We become more productive overall, as time off recharges our batteries. A long vacation once a year or, better yet, a slightly shorter vacation every six months goes a long way not only toward helping us make the most of our potential but also toward maintaining our psychological and physical well-being. As J. P. Morgan once remarked, "I can do a year's work in nine months, but not in twelve."

This does not mean that we cannot cope with difficult phases when marathon days, weeks, or even months are required. The birth of a new child, for example, leads to a period of intensity where recovery is a scarce commodity. Once in a while our work may present special challenges that demand extra effort from us. Our bodies and minds were created to handle such periods, at work or in our personal lives, provided there is recovery at the end of the marathon.

Many people wonder why it is that despite rising levels of material affluence, levels of depression and anxiety are so much higher today than they were thirty or forty years ago. One reason is simply that today there is greater awareness of mental health issues; many people are diagnosed today with a disorder that would have gone unnoticed a few decades ago. But that's not the entire story. The rise in suicide levels throughout the world clearly illustrates that there is an increase in the number of people confronting mental health problems. One major reason is that our lives have become significantly busier, and we have far fewer opportunities for recovery.

Growing up, I remember my parents having friends over on weekends as well as occasionally on weeknights. They would all sit around talking, eating, relaxing, and laughing. Today, my friends and I get together far less frequently, and when we do, we are often on the phone, checking our e-mail, generally distracted and restless. And we pay a price, because rather than recovering, we are adding to the stress.

We have a primal need for pleasure and recreation, but, as humans with free will, we can choose to ignore this need, to overcome our instincts and go against our nature. We convince ourselves that there is no limit to how far we can push ourselves, that just as science produces better, faster, more reliable and steady machines, we too can hone our abilities through modifying our nature. Adhering to the unconstrained view of human nature, we attempt to train ourselves to need less downtime—to sleep less, to rest less, to cease less—to do more and stretch ourselves beyond our limits. But, like it or not, there is a limit, and if we continue to violate nature's demands, to abuse ourselves, we will pay the price—individually and as a society.

The rising levels of mental health problems, coupled with improved psychiatric medication, are thrusting us toward a brave new world. To reverse direction, rather than listening to advertisers who promise us the wonder drug, the magic pill that will improve performance and mood, we need to listen to our nature and rediscover its wonders. Regular recovery, on the micro-, mid-, and macrolevels, can often do the work of psychiatric medicine, only naturally.

Introducing recovery in all aspects of my life has transformed my overall experience. In four or five intensive hour-and-a-half sessions, each followed by at least fifteen minutes of recovery, I get just about as much done as I did previously in a twelve-hour marathon day. Taking one full day off every week makes me more productive overall rather than less so. And finally, I have come to see vacations as both enjoyable and a good investment. As a sprinter today, I get as much work done as I did previously as a marathon runner—in a lot less time and with a lot more energy and positive emotions. I spend more time with my family and friends, and when I do, I am more present. There is no magic here; I am simply paying better attention to my human needs.

I'm off to meditate now. I suggest you take a break, too—perhaps a Time-In?

**TIME-IN** Are you getting enough recovery time? Do you take enough breaks during the day? Are you getting sufficient sleep each night? Do you take a day off once a week? When was your last vacation? When is the next one?

To my mind, the most important and exciting research in the area of organizational behavior explores how job satisfaction and job performance converge. They don't always converge; happier employees are not necessarily better employees. However, when it comes to perfectionism, the research is fairly clear: happiness and success *do* go together. In other words, not only are Optimalists more satisfied with their work, but their performance is generally better than that of Perfectionists.

There is much that a manager can do to bring out and reinforce the Optimalist in the employees. Instituting a psychologically safe environment leads to more learning and therefore to better long-term performance than an environment in which employees fear reporting failure. Instituting regular rest periods not only contributes to psychological health but also helps us achieve more.

Sounds like a good deal to me.

# EXERCISE

## ·•● Learning from Your Best Past

Write about a period—anywhere between a month and a year—when you thrived at work, when, in comparison to other times, you felt yourself most satisfied, productive, and creative. If you have not worked for long enough or cannot think of such a period, write about another time when you thrived—at school, for instance.

What was it about what you did then that led you to thrive? What form of recovery did you have in place? Whom did you work with? Most importantly, what can you learn from what you did then, and how can you apply it to what you are doing now or will be doing in the future?

In writing, commit to possible steps that you can take to work with people or in situations that bring out the best in you. In your date book, enter recovery sessions in the form of regular gym classes, outings with friends, and longer vacations with your family.

Just as you look at your own experiences, look at other people, at work or elsewhere. Ask yourself what you can learn from them, in terms of what you want to do and how you want to be, as well as in terms of what you would like to avoid.

# Optimal Love

---

**The course of true love never did run smooth.**

*—William Shakespeare*

A t this point in the book, having already shared with you much about myself, I would like to take self-disclosure a step further and admit that my favorite song is Whitney Houston's "And I Will Always Love You," with Celine Dion's "Let's Talk About Love" a close second. Of my top ten all-time favorites, eight are love songs (Beethoven's Ninth Symphony and Lee Ann Womack's "I Hope You Dance" somehow found their way onto that list). I love love. For as long as I breathe and my eyes can see, I will be moved by Shakespeare's words of devotion, and I will stay up, sleepless in Cambridge, watching Meg Ryan and Tom Hanks unite.

Like many others, I learned about romance from my favorite songs, poems, movies, and self-help books. And while one does not need to be a student of human relations to know that "love is the answer," finding the answer to the question "What is true love?" requires more than the ability to rhyme. It requires reason.

With the best of intentions, some poets, songwriters, movie directors, and relationship gurus have led us astray. They have depicted love as sweet, seductive, delightful, alluring. The trouble is that this image does not reflect reality and is potentially harmful. Here is an excerpt from one of the leading self-help writers of the twentieth century:

> Perfect love is rare indeed—for to be a lover will require that you continually have the subtlety of the very wise, the flexibility of the child, the sensitivity of the artist, the understanding of the philosopher, the acceptance of the saint, the tolerance of the scholar and the fortitude of the certain.[1]

This beautiful passage captures the essence of written words on love, spoken words on passion, and sung words on lust. So beautiful—and so harmful! Because, in fact, perfect love is not rare; it does not exist. Buying into the illusion that it does will lead to one of three outcomes. First, it may prevent us from ever finding a romantic partner, because we will always be waiting for that perfect person who has the flexibility of a child, the sensitivity of an artist, and so on. Second, we may decide to enter a relationship with a partner who does not have the qualities of a saint or philosopher, with the feeling that we have compromised, while continuing to seek, consciously or not, that perfect person. Finally, we may believe that we have found the perfect partner, only to feel profound disappointment and frustration when we discover our partner's flaws, as we inevitably will.

There certainly is a place, even a need, for writing, poetry, music, and films that depict the saintly and the beautiful. I have no doubt that more people make love after watching *Pride and Prejudice* or *Titanic* than they do after watching *Family Guy* or

*Married with Children.* And I certainly would refuse to relinquish 85 percent of my CD collection on the grounds that the songs are too romantic or that they fail to provide a fair representation of true love. The challenge is to come to terms with the fact that art is not (always) life, that our bedroom at home will differ—perhaps slightly, perhaps a great deal, but differ it will—from the film set where each perfect costume has been perfectly placed as it was perfectly torn from the lovers' perfect bodies. While something may be lost in translation from the movie set to our bedroom set, much more can be gained. What we need is love, like in the songs and movies and books and poems, only more—more real.

## Real Love

There comes a time in the course of every long-term relationship when we realize that our partner is not God's perfect gift to mankind, or womankind. Inevitably, the same realization sooner or later strikes our partner. We become fully aware for the first time of each other's flaws and imperfections, not in the superficial sense of perceiving these faults as cute or endearing but in a deep and sometimes troubling way. For example, we may realize that our partner has a streak of anger that we never noticed before or that he or she is gripped by insecurity and anxiety or has a tendency toward inconsistency and breaches of integrity. And even though we all know and accept and pay lip service to the idea that no one is perfect, facing the truth that our partner is no exception to this rule can be shocking and frightening.

The point of realization has parallels to the point when children understand that their parents are merely human—hence flawed—and they suddenly feel more alone and less secure in the world. A partner may then come along and take the place of our "perfect" parent. But the partner's eventual and inevitable fall from this perch of perfection—when his imperfections are exposed—can be more devastating to us than our realization that our parents are only human. In addition to our feeling more alone and insecure, our sense of judgment may be shaken as we realize that we were wrong about our partner—this time, unlike our earlier experience with our parents, without the excuse of childhood innocence. Our heart is broken and, worse, so are our reassuring illusions.

What happens at that point, when one or both partners wake up from the illusion of perfect love, is a crisis of confidence—in one's own judgment, in the judgment of one's partner, and in the future of the relationship. The crisis can signify either the beginning of the end of the relationship or the beginning of real love. One way or another, the relationship changes. It is transformed and can never be the same again.

While not all relationships should or can be sustained, while not all partners are compatible, the dissolution or deterioration of most relationships is avoidable. To realize the potential inherent in the relationship, it is necessary to accept that there are flaws in the partner and in the partnership. Needless to say, accepting flaws does not mean being resigned to them; a willingness by both partners to work on their failings is a prerequisite for a flourishing relationship. The healthy approach is one of active acceptance, which means that before we start working to improve what needs to be improved, there has to be a fundamental acceptance that these flaws exist.

The Perfectionist who has been forced to recognize that his partner is flawed may shift from one extreme and unrealistic view (that his partner is perfect) to an equally extreme and unrealistic view (that his partner is completely flawed). When, for example, a Perfectionist becomes aware of a jealous streak in his partner, his perception of the partner may shift radically and sometimes instantaneously, from loving and caring to obsessive and smothering. Accepting human flaws as a fact of life, which is the way of the Optimalist, creates the space within which the nuances and complexities that are part of every relationship can exist.

The expectations that we have of our partner and the promise that love holds are important in creating a thriving partnership. At the same time, these expectations must be realistic or else they will lead to disappointment and frustration. While it is pleasant—exalting, even—to be admired by your partner as the epitome of perfection, it is also liberating not to be placed on a pedestal. Of course, this feeling of liberation comes only if the loss of the illusion is replaced with loving acceptance. This will not happen instantaneously, but acceptance has to emerge for the relationship to thrive. Acceptance is not a call for mediocrity, for compromise, but rather a prerequisite for the attainment of optimal success and happiness on a personal as well as interpersonal level.

**TIME-IN** Do you accept the flaws in your partner? If there are flaws that you find difficult to accept, are they related to flaws in yourself that you do not accept?

The impact of perfectionism begins even before a relationship starts. The Perfectionist's fear of failure—manifested, in the context of romantic relations, in a fear of rejection—prevents the Perfectionist from trying to initiate relationships, from making the first move, unless she is certain that her interest will be reciprocated. Not only is the Perfectionist concerned about being rejected, but she also has unrealistic expectations of potential partners. The all-or-nothing mind-set magnifies every imperfection into a deal breaker and prevents potential relationships from ever taking off. And then, once the relationship takes off, every bump, every disagreement, every conflict is catastrophized and experienced as a potential relationship-ending threat.

## And They Quarreled Happily Ever After . . .

In many romantic movies, the protagonists fight and quarrel—this is necessary in order to hold the audience's attention—but then after ninety minutes or so, they resolve their disagreements, they kiss passionately, and from then on (we are led to believe) it's smooth sailing into the sunset and the happily ever after. It happened to Mr. and Mrs. Smith, it happened repeatedly to Katharine Hepburn and Spencer Tracy, and even Wall-E and Eve show us that that is what love's about.

Of course, this pattern is the opposite of what usually happens in real relationships. The initial stages of a relationship—courtship, marriage, honeymoon phase—are often relatively conflict free. But then, for as long as the couple is together, there is conflict. To many, conflict within a relationship means that the relationship itself is in trouble; perfect harmony—the absence of conflict—is considered the standard we should all strive for. The Perfectionist assumes that the initial stages of the relationship should be used to iron out all potential disagreements in preparation for the smooth ride ahead, just like in the movies. Just as the Perfectionist expects her partner to be flawless, so she expects the relationship to be conflict free.

As it turns out, conflict is not only unavoidable but is actually crucial for the long-term success of the relationship. Psychologist John Gottman, who has, for many years, researched thriving and failing relationships, has shown that couples in successful long-term relationships enjoy a five-to-one ratio between positive and negative events.[2] For every expression of anger or criticism or hostility, there are five instances where the partners act kindly to each other, show empathy, make love, express interest, or display affection toward one another.

While Gottman found Aristotle's golden mean to be around the five-to-one ratio point, we should keep in mind that the ratio is an average across many relationships. There are successful relationships where the ratio is three to one and others where it is ten to one. The key messages from Gottman's research are, first, that some negativity is vital and, second, that it is essential to have more positivity than negativity. Little or no conflict within a relationship indicates that the partners are not dealing with important issues and differences. Given that no person or partnership is perfect, absence of conflict indicates that the partners are avoiding challenges, running away from confrontations rather than learning from them. At the same time, while conflict is important, relationships that do not contain significantly more kindness and affection than harshness and anger are unhealthy.

Another element that Gottman emphasizes is that not all conflicts are alike. Some couples are quiet and never raise their voices, whereas others thrive on volatility; for the former, an annoyed or a disappointed look may be an expression of negativity, while the latter may show their displeasure by gesticulating wildly and throwing plates across the room. Long-term relationships that fall into either category can succeed, as long as partners are generally careful to separate the person from the behavior. Doing so is as important in the living room or the bedroom as it is in the classroom or the boardroom.

It is healthy for partners to challenge one another's words and behaviors, if there is unconditional acceptance at the heart of the relationship. What is most destructive for a relationship, Gottman found, is hostility—an attack on the person—be it in the form of name-calling, insults, hurtful sarcasm, or other ways of putting the partner down. Telling your partner that he is an inconsiderate slob is an attack on the person; telling him how it upsets you to enter a smelly kitchen after you had agreed that he would take out the garbage is focusing on the behavior.

To make matters worse, more and more couples engage in public displays of contention. Sanctioned by our culture of reality shows that have brought voyeurism to prime-time television, many couples feel comfortable airing their dirty laundry in public. Strife, when public, adds humiliation to the equation, embarrassing not only the person being chastised but also those who are forced to witness the interaction. In essence, what a relationship needs is basic respect and common courtesy.

Gottman's advice to couples, beyond striving to higher levels of respect and acceptance, is that they should accentuate the positive aspects of the relationship. Accentuating the positive does not necessarily require radical change and transformation. Just as architect Ludwig Mies van der Rohe once asserted that "God is in the details," so have relationship researchers illustrated that love is in the details. Lasting love is not founded on the lavish one-week cruise or the nine carat diamond but rather on the day-to-day, ordinary expressions of love.

Peter Fraenkel of the Ackerman Institute for the Family recommends introducing "sixty-second pleasure points." Fraenkel suggests that rather than relying primarily on special events or special gifts to sustain a relationship, each partner should initiate as few as three pleasure points each day. A passionate kiss, a thoughtful or funny e-mail or an amorous text message, a simple "I love you"—all these can go a long way toward sustaining and cultivating love. Heartfelt compliments are important, too. Mark Twain once quipped that he could live for two months on a good compliment. If we fail to appreciate the positive in our relationship, then the positive, instead of appreciating, will depreciate.

Compliments and other forms of accentuating the positive are not merely pleasant in and of themselves, they also amount to a good long-term investment. Just as depositing money in a savings account when things are going well can generate interest and can help us weather financial difficulties, so can positive actions committed regularly generate goodwill and help a couple weather hard times within the relationship.

**TIME-IN** Come up with a list of sixty-second pleasure points, and, in writing, commit to doing at least three of them per day for the next week. They can be different ones or the same ones each day.

Conflicts, like positive acts, can strengthen a relationship. Think of daily conflicts as a form of vaccine. When we inoculate against a disease, we are in fact injecting a weakened strain of the disease into the body, which is then stimulated to develop the antibodies that enable it to deal with more major assaults later on. Likewise, minor conflicts help our relationship develop defense capabilities; they immunize the relationship and subsequently help partners deal with major conflicts when they arise.

There are parallels between a conflict-free relationship and an overprotected baby. A newborn baby who is placed in a sterilized environment for a year will be less resilient and more vulnerable later on in life than one who has been living in the "dirty" real-world environment. Children who grow up on farms and are exposed to more dirt and germs than their more urban counterparts develop stronger immune systems and are less likely to have allergies and asthma later in life. Failures, conflicts, and hardships are important for cultivating resilience, both physically and psychologically.

As couples continue to have conflicts—alongside positive interactions—they build up the immune system of their relationship.

## Gridlock

According to sex therapist David Schnarch, sooner or later, every long-term relationship experiences what he refers to as gridlock, the point at which couples feel stuck in a conflict and see no way out.[3] This is not just a regular conflict that is easily resolved or forgotten but an intense and recurring conflict that seems unsolvable. These recurring conflicts usually revolve around issues relating to children, in-laws, money, or sex. What kind of education should the children receive? What is the desirable frequency of sexual relations, and what turns each partner on? Gridlock often challenges the sense of self of one or both partners, because it confronts them with a choice between integrity (holding on to their beliefs) and getting along with their partner by compromising.

It is not uncommon for relationships that reach gridlock to come to an end. The partners may divorce, or, if for one reason or another they choose to remain legally bound, they may be spiritually, physically, and emotionally apart. What Schnarch suggests, though, is that gridlock is a critical point, an opportunity for personal and interpersonal growth: "Marriage operates at much greater intensity and pressure than we expect—so great, in fact, couples mistakenly assume it's time for divorce when it's really time to get to work." Partners who successfully overcome gridlock emerge stronger as individuals and as a couple; their relationship becomes more authentic and intimate.

One of the most important ways of cultivating intimacy and depth within a relationship—of getting to know, and to be known by, our partner—is through dealing with interpersonal problems, which Schnarch refers to as "the drive wheels and grind stones of intimate relationships." The mere realization that conflicts—from minor disagreements to major gridlock—are not only inevitable but also beneficial is liberating and can potentially take away some of the threat that a Perfectionist experiences with each bump in the road. Deviations from the straight line are not indicative of an inherent flaw in one of the partners or the relationship but rather are part of the process, with the general direction being toward greater acceptance, intimacy, and passion.

# Sex

Schnarch, whose work has revolutionized the area of marriage counseling and sex therapy, points out that sex can actually get better with time. As Schnarch puts it, "Cellulite and sexual potential are highly correlated." Our potential to peak sexually is greater when we are in our fifties or sixties, and sex with the partner we've been with for decades can be significantly better than with a new person. This flies in the face of conventional wisdom. After all, sexual arousal is generally higher at twenty-four than at sixty-four, and our physical reaction is more pronounced when encountering a sexy stranger than it is when we see our partner of three decades. However, as Schnarch points out, great sex is not the product of the immediate biological, physiological response to our partner; great sex combines our hearts and minds in addition to our bodies.

Schnarch compares *"genital prime*—the peak years of physical reproductive maturity—with *sexual prime*—the specifically human capacity for adult eroticism and emotional connection." And when it comes to sexual prime, older can be better: "If you want intimacy during sex, there isn't a 16-year-old that can keep up with a healthy 60-year-old. People are capable of much better sex and intimacy as they mature."

In terms of Carol Dweck's fixed and growth mind-sets that I described earlier, we can understand Schnarch's perspective as a growth mind-set: sex potentially improves over time, as we become more intimate—more comfortable, more at home, more open, more accepting—with our partner and, no less importantly, with ourselves. The fixed mind-set in relation to sex would be the notion that sexual capabilities and performance are immutable, unchanging—I am either good in bed or I am not, we are either a good fit or we are not.

Because after a certain age there is gradual physical decline—the fifty-year-old body cannot do everything that a body half its age is capable of—the person who does not recognize the difference between sex as a purely physical act and sex as encompassing both mind and body may assume a decline mind-set. While the growth mind-set suggests that sex gets better with time and the fixed mind-set that sex does not change, the person with the decline mind-set expect that sex will get worse over time. The decline mind-set takes away from the joy of sex and becomes a self-fulfilling prophecy—sex really does get worse.

Understanding that love can intensify with time and that, with it, sex can improve takes us from a decline or a fixed mind-set to a growth mind-set, from the Perfectionist's way of thinking to the Optimalist's. Deviations from the straight line—an imperfect performance in the bedroom, a heated argument, or a cold exchange—are not indicative of a tragic flaw but rather part of the natural flow toward a better, more intimate relationship. The fixed mind-set leads to the all-or-nothing approach, where each imperfection is catastrophized. The growth mind-set, in contrast, allows for imperfection in oneself, in one's partner, and in the relationship.

**TIME-IN** What do you need to do to bring more joy to the bedroom? What do you need to let go of?

## Help Meet

As I discussed in earlier chapters, one of the most dominant characteristics of Perfectionists is their defensiveness. Needless to say, it is very difficult to cultivate intimacy when one or both partners immediately go on the attack when they are criticized. By refusing to accept criticism, Perfectionists lose the opportunity to gain insight into themselves and to grow.

In the King James Version of the Hebrew Bible, God says, after creating the first man, that "it is not good that man should be alone, I will make him an *help meet* for him." In this context, the word *meet* means "competition" or "encounter," as in athletic meet or a meeting of the minds. *Help meet* is a translation of the Hebrew phrase *ezer kenegdo*, literally meaning "help against him."

The phrase *ezer kenegdo* has caused biblical translators and commentators much anguish. How could it be that a benevolent God created the woman to oppose man? To resolve the apparent contradiction, later translations replaced *help meet* with the phrase *help alongside*. Some commentators explain the phrase to mean that if a man is righteous, his wife will be his help, and if he sins, his wife will be against him. I would suggest, though, that the phrase be taken at face value—help can truly come through opposition. It is within a help-meet relationship that the man and the woman challenge one another, each helping the other attain greater heights.

In his revolutionary work *The Subjection of Women*, nineteenth-century English philosopher John Stuart Mill called for the liberation of women.[4] He argued that "the principle which regulates the existing social relations between the two sexes—the legal subordination of one sex to the other—is wrong in itself, and now one of the chief hindrances to human improvement." Only when a man and a woman are equal can they "enjoy the luxury of looking up to the other, and can have alternately the pleasure of leading and of being led in the path of development." In healthy relationships, the man and the woman, at different times, take the lead and further the development of their partner.

The notion of leading and being led, of a help-meet partnership, applies not only to the relationship between a man and a woman but to any other intimate relationship. In his essay "Friendship," Ralph Waldo Emerson recognized opposition as a necessary precondition for a friendship. In a friend, Emerson wrote, he was not looking for a "mush of concessions" or "trivial conveniency"—in other words, for someone who would agree with everything he said. Rather, he was looking for a "*beautiful enemy*, untamable, devoutly revered."[5] The philosopher Edmund Burke echoed Emerson's sentiments about relationships: "He that wrestles with us strengthens our nerves, and sharpens our skill. Our antagonist is our helper."[6]

A person who only wants to be "beautiful" and supportive toward me without ever resisting or challenging what I do and say does not push me to improve and grow; a person who disputes what I say and do without caring and supporting me is antagonistic and harsh. A true friend will be both beautiful toward me and behave as an "enemy." A beautiful enemy challenges my behavior and my words and at the same time unconditionally accepts my person. A beautiful enemy is someone who respects and loves me enough to question my ideas and behaviors; at the same time, her opposition to any of my words or actions does not change how much she cares for me as a person.

TIME-IN Who are the beautiful enemies in your life? In what ways have they helped you? How can you become more of a beautiful enemy to others?

My wife, Tami, and I have had our fair share of disagreements and disputes—and will undoubtedly continue to have them. We have encountered minor conflicts and have had to deal with major gridlock. But as a result of confronting these issues and resolving them, our relationship has become stronger and we have matured individually and as a couple. Why? Because underneath the hurt, frustration, irritation, or fear there is always a strong desire to learn and grow and make our relationship better.

We dislike conflicts and certainly do not seek them out; but when they find us, we plunge into the storm. And when we reach the ominous stillness in the eye of the storm—the point of realization and recognition, the point of knowing and of clear seeing—we hold one another and together, leading or being led, make it out to safer shores. Conflicts do not necessarily happen for the best, but we are learning to make the best of conflicts that happen.

# EXERCISE

## ●●● Sentence Completion

Complete the following sentence stems as quickly as possible; try not to think too much before you write. Then read them over and consider what you can learn about yourself and your relationships. Some of the stems relate to a particular person (for X, write the name of a person you care about), and others focus on relationships in general.

To improve my relationship with X by 5 percent . . .

If I open myself up 5 percent more . . .

To create more intimacy in my relationship . . .

If I accept X 5 percent more . . .

If I accept myself 5 percent more . . .

To improve the relationship I have with myself . . .

To bring more love to my life . . .

I am beginning to see that . . .

# Part 3

# MEDITATIONS

# 8

# First Meditation: Real Change

It's not that some people have willpower and
some don't. It's that some people are ready to
change and others are not.

—*James Gordon*

An experiment conducted by Ellen Langer and her student
Loralyn Thompson helped me understand why the shift
from perfectionism to optimalism has been so difficult for
me and for others.[1] Participants in the study were given a list of
undesirable traits, such as rigid, gullible, and grim, and were then
asked which of these traits they had tried to change in themselves
and whether or not they had succeeded. Later, they were asked to
evaluate the importance of traits such as consistency, trust, and
seriousness. What participants were unaware of was that the traits
on the second list are often seen as the positive equivalents of the
traits on the first list. Consistency may be perceived as the positive
version of rigidity, being trusting may be seen as the positive side
of gullibility.

What Langer found was that those who valued a certain positive trait had difficulty changing its negative counterpart—those

who valued consistency, for example, had difficulty becoming less rigid because deep down, subconsciously, they feared it would mean becoming less consistent.

Along similar lines, people do not give up excessive feelings of guilt because they do not want to lose their sensitivity; they continue to worry out of proportion to the situations they are dealing with, because they fear that not worrying will mean not being responsible. Then there are those who remain faultfinders because they believe that being a benefit finder implies being detached from reality. As Langer writes, "The reason some people have a hard time changing their behavior, no matter how hard they seem to try, is that they really value that behavior under a different name."

**TIME-IN** Can you think of any traits or behaviors that you have tried to change and haven't been able to? Are there positive counterparts to those traits that you value and do not want to lose?

One of the reasons perfectionism is difficult to overcome is because we associate it with certain positive traits. Many people in job interviews mention perfectionism when they are asked to name a personal weakness. They usually equate perfectionism with making sure things are done and done well and paying attention to details. Their "admission" of perfectionism is a roundabout way of revealing a strength, of saying, "I am detail oriented, methodical, hard working, and you can trust me."

Why was it so difficult for me to change my perfectionism, even though I knew that it was making me unhappy? Because although I saw perfectionism as problematic, I also associated it with being meticulous and driven. And because I didn't want to be sloppy and lazy, I chose—or my subconscious chose for me—to remain a Perfectionist, despite the price I knew I was paying.

To be able to change, we need a nuanced understanding of what exactly it is that we want to get rid of and what we want to keep. Researcher Dina Nir writes about the importance of unbundling, the process of taking a particular quality and separating it into "two or more distinct and explicitly defined sub-aspects."[2] There are a number of characteristics that are bundled within perfectionism, and to bring about change we have to unbundle them—to understand which we want to keep and which we don't.

To apply the unbundling process to the trait of perfectionism, we can start by asking some or all of the questions that Nir suggests: What does perfectionism mean to me? What do I gain from being a Perfectionist? What aspects of perfectionism am I proud of? What price do I pay for being a Perfectionist? What price do others pay for my perfectionism? Which aspects of perfectionism do I want to keep? Which elements of perfectionism do I want to get rid of?

In my own case, while I want to rid myself of my fear of failure and my rejection of painful emotions (which psychologists associate with negative, maladaptive perfectionism), I want to keep my drive and ambition (which I associate with optimalism). Once I define those areas where I want to change and those where I do not, I am likely to be less conflicted and consequently more ready to change. After we unbundle the traits, we can decide whether or not we want to change and, if we do, what exactly it is that we want to change. Essentially, what Langer's study suggests—whether we apply it to perfectionism, rigidity, faultfinding, or any other trait or behavior—is a shift from the Perfectionist's all-or-nothing approach to a more nuanced, realistic analysis.

# EXERCISE

## Unbundling Perfectionism

List some of the characteristics or behaviors that you would like to change but have been unable to up to now—for instance, being overly anxious or being a Perfectionist or being too busy. Write down some positive traits associated with each one. For example, if you see yourself as someone who worries too much about everything, positive traits you associate with this might be "feeling concerned about others" or "having a developed sense of responsibility." Or you might think of "being driven" and "getting a lot done" as positive sides of "being too busy." In writing, elaborate on what it is that you want to change and what you would like to keep.

# 9

# Second Meditation: Cognitive Therapy

Your emotions follow your thoughts, just as surely as baby ducks follow their mother. But the fact that the baby ducks follow faithfully along doesn't prove that the mother knows where she is going!

—*David Burns*

The cognitive revolution that was launched in the 1960s took the psychology world by storm, challenging the two schools that dominated twentieth-century psychology: psychoanalysis and behaviorism. Psychoanalysts primarily focused on subconscious drives and defenses in trying to understand patients and enhance their quality of life. Behaviorists focused on external forces such as reward and punishment to explain and modify behaviors and experiences. Cognitive psychologists came along and, while still acknowledging the roles of both the subconscious and conditioning, shifted their focus to the conscious mind— our thoughts, ideas, and judgments. Cognitive therapists introduced concepts such as choice and agency into the psychological vocabulary, differentiating themselves both from psychoanalysts (who believe that we are primarily slaves to our instincts or early experiences) and from behaviorists (who view humans primarily in terms of their reactions to their external environment).

While there is much evidence illustrating the positive effect of psychoanalysis and behavior-based therapy, more than forty years of research shows that cognitive therapy is at least as effective as, and usually more effective than, the two older schools of therapy. Cognitive therapeutic techniques are relatively straightforward, and, while ideally they should be learned and implemented with the help of a qualified therapist, the fundamentals can provide some benefit to most people even without direct professional guidance.

The basic premise of cognitive therapy is that we react to our interpretation of events rather than directly to the events themselves, which is why the same event may elicit radically different responses from different people. An event leads to a thought (an interpretation of the event), and the thought in turn evokes an emotion. I see a baby (event), recognize her as my daughter (thought), and feel love (emotion). I see the audience waiting for my lecture (event), interpret it as threatening (thought), and experience anxiety (emotion).

Event ⟶ Thought ⟶ Emotion

Research in cognitive therapy suggests that much of the emotional pain that we experience is avoidable, as it is caused by distorted thinking and irrational thoughts. If you ask someone on a date and are rejected (event), and you conclude that no one will ever want you (thought), with the result that you feel devastated for months (emotion), you are being irrational, and your emotional response is disproportionate and unhelpful. If, following the same event, you conclude that a particular person is not interested in you (thought) and you feel sad (emotion), you are being rational and your emotional response is proportionate and helpful.

The goal of cognitive therapy is to restore a sense of realism by getting rid of distorted thinking. When we identify an irrational thought (a cognitive distortion), we change the way we think about an event and thereby change the way we feel. For example, if I experience paralyzing anxiety before a job interview, I can evaluate the thought that elicits the anxiety (if I am rejected, it will all be over and I will never find a job) and reinterpret the event by disputing and replacing the distorted evaluation with a rational one (although I really want this job, there are many other desirable jobs out there). The distortion elicits an intense and unhealthy fear of failure; the rational thought reframes the situation and puts it in perspective.

TIME-IN Reflect on an intense emotional reaction that you have had to a particular situation. Was your reaction appropriate? Is there another way of interpreting the situation?

## The PRP Process

One of the most useful methods that I have found for dealing with disturbing emotions associated with failure, whether it is fear of failure or the agony of having made a mistake, is to follow the PRP process: giving myself the *permission* to be human, *reconstructing* the situation, and gaining a wider *perspective*.

**Permission.** An emotion is an emotion, whether it is based on rational or irrational thoughts, on a correct evaluation of reality or a distorted view. To deal with an emotion in a healthy manner, the first step we need to take is to accept it as part of our reality, just as we accept the law of gravity. In addition to accepting the emotion, we also need to accept the reality of the event that elicited the emotion. Fighting reality, pretending that we are not feeling what we are feeling or that what happened didn't really happen, only intensifies the painful emotion. To grant our emotions permission to be, it helps to write about whatever it is that we are feeling. We can also simply sit down and experience the emotion or observe its physical manifestation and accept it.

**Reconstruction.** Once we have truly accepted the reality of the situation and our emotions, we are ready to move on to cognitive reconstruction. This is where we change our interpretation of an event from a negative/unhelpful interpretation to a positive/helpful one.

Psychologist Joe Tomaka and his colleagues have demonstrated that the same event can elicit different physiological responses depending on whether we perceive it as a threat or a challenge.[1] Over time, we can train our mind to gravitate toward interpreting events as challenging rather than as threatening. When I feel excessively anxious before a speaking engagement, I often reconstruct my assessment of the event from a threat to a challenge. I try to do the same with other events as well, changing my evaluation of them from, say, an obligation to a privilege or from a test to an adventure.

We can also change our interpretation retrospectively, after things have not turned out quite as we expected or hoped they would. By asking ourselves what we can learn from a particular failure, for instance, and how we have grown or can grow as a result, we can reconstruct our perception of the event. Though we may still feel disappointed that things didn't turn out the way we had hoped they would, we can remind ourselves that no significant journey, no matter how successful the eventual outcome, is free of failure—that, as Thomas Watson said, to increase our success rate we need to double our failure rate. We can become benefit finders rather than faultfinders and recognize that while things do not necessarily happen for the best, some people are able to make the best of the things that happen.

**Perspective.** Wayne Dyer and Richard Carlson's advice not to sweat the small stuff is invaluable.[2] Often, when we look at a situation in its broader context, our worries and disappointments diminish. Realistically, will getting the B on the exam shatter my chances of ever making something of my life? Probably not. A year from now, will the fact that I stumbled over a few lines in my speech really matter? Probably not. We can also look at the bigger picture by appreciating all the wonderful things in our life, which, taken together, eclipse the particular experience that was painful.

Reconstructing a situation or gaining perspective is not about avoiding all painful emotions. Some unpleasant feelings are appropriate. The right time to use cognitive reconstruction or to remind ourselves not to sweat the small stuff is when our emotions are disproportionate to the situation.

I use the PRP process for dealing with painful emotions in general and with emotions related to perfectionism in particular. For instance, a few days ago, I intended to get some writing done between dropping my daughter off at day care and teaching a class. But by the time I left home with Shirelle, I realized that it was late and that I would not get any writing done that morning. I got very upset with myself for not being more efficient—for not living up to my expectations. So I applied the PRP process.

First, I gave myself the *permission* to be human, to experience the disappointment and frustration that I felt. I did not punish myself for feeling the way I did but accepted my emotions as they were. I then *reconstructed* the situation, seeking the positive, which in this case was that the experience helped me realize that I was too busy generally, and that I needed to limit my obligations in order to enjoy the things that were important to me, like spending time with my daughter or writing. Finally, I shifted my *perspective* and reminded myself that in a year from now—or, most likely, in just a week from now—that extra hour of writing won't matter much. Instead of racing home to try to get some writing done, I took my time with my daughter: we had a leisurely walk outside her day care before I dropped her off.

Applying the PRP process is a skill, and like any skill it requires practice. Initially, working through the three stages may seem artificial. However, after a while the process feels more natural, and it can help with both mild and intense emotions, for situations involving rational as well as irrational thoughts. With some intense emotions, you may find that you need to spend a lot of time in the permission mode. In other situations, simply acknowledging the emotion may be enough, and you will be able to move on immediately to the next stage.

# EXERCISE

## The PRP Process

Think of a recent event that has upset you emotionally or of an upcoming event that you are worried about. Begin by giving yourself the *permission* to be human: acknowledge what happened as well as the emotion that you are feeling as a result. You can write about or talk about how you feel, or, if you prefer, give yourself the time and space to experience the experience. This stage can last five seconds or five minutes or more.

*Reconstruct* the situation. Ask yourself what positive outcomes this situation can have. This does not mean that you are happy about it, but simply that there are benefits that can be derived. Can you learn something new? Can you gain a new insight into yourself or others? Can you become more empathetic or more appreciative of what you have in life?

Finally, take a step back and gain a wider *perspective* on the situation. Can you see the experience in the larger scheme of things? How will you see the situation a year from now? Are you sweating the small stuff?

Progressing through the PRP process does not have to be linear: you can move from permission to perspective, then to reconstruction, then back to permission again, and so on.

Repeat this exercise on a regular basis, either by actively looking for an experience that happened or by responding to experiences as they happen. The more you practice, the more benefit you will derive from it.

# 10

# Third Meditation: Imperfect Advice

In my early professional years I was asking the question: How can I treat, or cure, or change this person? Now I would phrase the question in this way: How can I provide a relationship which this person may use for his own personal growth?

—*Carl Rogers*

I am a problem solver. In high school, my favorite subject was math. The clarity, the certainty, the sense of closure I got when I solved a math problem—these were the elements that attracted me to working with numbers. In college my interests changed, as the personal challenges that I faced with my perfectionism and stress drew me away from figures and toward trying to figure out the human psyche—specifically, initially, my own. But while the content of my studies changed (from numbers to people), the methodology did not, and I still sought the same clarity and closure.

My goal was to make myself and others happier, and to me that was all about finding solutions to problems. One day, when I was a graduate student, a friend took me to lunch and told me that he had been going through a rough time. He was no longer sure he was in the right field, he was unable to motivate himself, and instead of working he was spending most of his time procrastinating. I listened to him for a few minutes and then launched into a monologue in which I analyzed his problem, and then, with certainty and conviction, provided him a clear and simple solution.

I told him about some writing exercises that could help him identify his passions and, potentially, an alternative career path. I shared with him some motivational theory and then suggested a few steps that he could take to overcome procrastination—a topic I was well versed in, having studied and taught it for a number of years. Pure reason, very scientific, very insightful—and totally unhelpful.

Throughout the conversation, as I was sharing my experience and expertise, I felt that he was not really listening, that my words were not getting through. I tried harder, explained better, rephrased my suggestions, and generated more practical exercises and creative ideas, but to no avail. It was only later that day, when I had time to reflect on our conversation, that I realized that what he needed was not my solution but my presence; he didn't need my theories, just a sympathetic ear.

According to Carl Rogers, the role of the therapist (or anyone else in a helping relationship) is to create an environment of unconditional positive regard for the client. In Rogerian therapy, the psychologist does little more than reflect back what the client says and provide a safe environment in which the client feels accepted and therefore comfortable being himself. Over time the client internalizes the therapist's unconditional positive regard and becomes stronger, better able to deal with challenges and difficulties on his own. "My aim," writes Rogers, "has been to provide a climate which contains as much of safety, of warmth, of empathic understanding, as I can genuinely find in myself to give."[1]

Robyn Dawes, in his book *House of Cards*, draws on the substantial research in the area of therapy to illustrate how the efficacy of a therapist, once she has the basic skills and knowledge, is not determined by the number or type of degrees she has earned but by the degree of empathy that she has. Empathy allows us to put ourselves in the other person's shoes and to understand what the person truly needs. I am more likely to be empathetic to the person before me when I am truly listening to him without being distracted by thoughts about how to advise him. The foundation of effective therapy is not only intellectual sophistication and knowledge but the ability to accept and to empathize.

While coming up with solutions to a friend's problems may make us feel helpful and competent, it often has the opposite effect on the friend. First, offering solutions creates distance between two people: one person is in the know (above), the other is in trouble (below). Second, the person being helped feels inadequate, especially when he is already feeling weak. When we offer solutions, regardless of our intentions, the message often comes across as condescending and paternalistic.

But when we embrace and accept, we communicate a different set of messages. First, and most importantly, we are telling the person, "I am with you. I care about you, and you can count on me." Second, we are telling him, "I trust you. You are smart enough and competent enough to get through this." When the mode is one of acceptance, even though it is clear that one person is helping and the other is being helped, the latter is more likely to feel understood and empowered. It is not always easy to refrain from giving advice, especially when we are with people we care about, but advice is not always the best thing we have to offer. Usually, simply being there is sufficient.

There are times when suggesting a solution is appropriate. If, for example, my friend is struggling with procrastination, it may be useful for me to share my expertise in this area—but only after I have listened to him. In the interpersonal domain—just as in the intrapersonal domain—we need active acceptance: first accept, be there for him, and only then provide advice and suggest solutions. There are, unfortunately, no simple rules that tell us when to embrace and when to try to help actively. This is where empathy comes in. An empathetic therapist or friend senses when acceptance is sufficient and when it may be helpful to offer suggestions.

While Perfectionists are inclined to give advice and fix things—to make things perfect again—they are equally disinclined to ask for advice or any kind of help. In fact, one of the best ways for Perfectionists to move toward optimalism is to actively ask for help—to reach out, to show a need, to be vulnerable. Initially, it may feel awkward and difficult, but as is true for any new behavior, one gets used to it. Personally, one of the most significant benefits that I have received from being in a long-term intimate relationship, one that is based on mutual trust, has been learning to ask for help and, through it, gaining the strength to be weak. I have taken that understanding to other relationships and situations in my life.

**TIME-IN** Is there something you need help with? Can you reach out to someone you trust for help?

A human being is not a series of mathematical formulas, where we can just plug in the right number in place of a particular variable and the problem is solved. The human psyche, especially when troubled or weak, needs sensitivity and care more than it does solutions and advice. For it is out of this soft embrace, the nurturing soil of acceptance, that the full strength and power and force of the person can emerge.

# EXERCISE

## Learning from Another Person

Think of a particular person who has helped you, or is helping you, through difficult times. Write about the person and specifically about what he or she does that is so helpful. Write about a particular conversation with this person that helped you or a particular event in which this person gave you strength.

What can you learn from the way the person acts or talks? What can you apply to your own attempts to help others? You can repeat this exercise by thinking of one or two more people and then identifying the thread that is common to those who have helped you.

# 11

# Fourth Meditation: A Perfect New World

---

**To foster a society of total happiness is to concoct a culture of fear.**

—*Eric Wilson*

Aldous Huxley in *Brave New World* described a future in which emotional pain is eradicated through the use of a wonder drug, Soma. Less than a century after its publication in 1932, Huxley's chilling account of an emotionally sterile world does not seem that far-fetched.

It is a natural and healthy part of our constitution to seek pleasure and avoid pain, but technological advances that provide us a glimpse of a brave new world are taking this healthy drive to an unhealthy extreme. We have become a culture obsessed with perfect pleasure, and we believe that a happy and fulfilling life is devoid of painful emotions. Any discomfort that breaks, or threatens to break, the flawless flow of positive emotions is taken as a sign of some inherent fault, one that must be fixed quickly.

The blame for this misunderstanding of what human happiness means lies, at least in part, with the medical establishment. Too many in the medical profession have taken the notion of "seek pleasure and avoid pain" to its simplistic extreme and dispense medication at the slightest hint of emotional discomfort. The ease with which psychiatric medication is dispensed today communicates, in deeds more than in words, the prevailing belief that all painful emotions should be done away with.

While there are certainly situations in which medication is appropriate—lives have been saved thanks to advances in psychiatry—there are far more situations in which it is not. Last semester one of my students was devastated after he received his first-ever B, and after thirty minutes in the doctor's office—the first time he had ever visited a psychiatrist—he was prescribed an antidepressant.

Barring extreme situations when, for instance, suicidal thoughts and feelings are involved, painful emotions should not be so readily medicated away. A student who is miserable because he failed an exam does not need to be put on medication; he needs to learn to deal with failure (or perceived failure). A person who has just been through a breakup does not need antidepressants; he needs to grieve. An employee who just lost her job is not helped in the long run if her emotions are suppressed by chemicals; she will benefit a great deal if she works through her painful feelings. In a manner of speaking, emotions are the printout of the soul. Over time, we can learn to read them, to understand the message that they contain, and to take appropriate action.

To give a personal example, over the years I have come to realize that when for no apparent reason I experience deep sadness and a sense of futility, it is usually because I have too much on my plate. I push myself to the limit, taking on too many responsibilities and not letting go of anything for fear that I might miss out on something. And then I get a message of sorts, through my emotions, telling me to stop, to slow down, to simplify my life, to recover. I could, of course, medicate away the sadness and continue working just as much or more, which is what many people today choose to do. But the voice of my emotions is too important, and to mute it would ultimately hurt me and those around me.

**TIME-IN** Think about a painful emotion that you are currently experiencing or one that you have recently experienced. What can you learn from the feeling?

In *The Matrix*, Neo, the movie's protagonist, is offered the choice between a red and a blue pill. The red pill would reveal the truth—a painful truth—about human existence. The blue pill would leave Neo in a state of happy oblivion, not knowing that he is in fact living in a make-believe world where he is kept sedated by the forces that have taken over our world. Neo chooses the red pill, faces the harsh reality head-on, and embarks on an odyssey that includes the pain of grief and failure, as well as the joy of discovery and development.

Would I have chosen a life without perfectionism had the choice been presented to me when I first became aware of the price I was paying as an athlete, a student, a writer, a partner? Possibly. Would I have chosen a life without perfectionism had I known what I would gain by struggling through it, the growth that would take place alongside the real emotional pain? Absolutely not.

Today, advances in the development of psychopharmaceuticals are making this sort of choice a reality. In *Against Happiness*, author Eric Wilson writes, "Soon, perhaps, with the help of psychopharmaceuticals, we shall have no more unhappy people in our country. Melancholics will become unknown."[1]

Sometime in the not-too-distant future we, our children, or our grandchildren will be given a quick and easy option—in the form of a pill or through genetic reprogramming—to do away with the fear of failure, to circumvent painful emotions, and to inject our lives with a sense of accomplishment. I hope that future generations will choose the red pill or, better yet, no pill at all.

# EXERCISE

## ·•● Focused Journaling

In the second meditation I discussed cognitive therapy and its potential benefits. Research has shown that when it comes to dealing with the psychological fallout of perfectionism—be it anxiety or depression—cognitive therapy interventions are as effective as, and at times more effective than, medicine. The following simple exercise, if done on a regular basis, can change the way we interpret events and thus our emotional reaction to events.

Create a table with three columns. In the first column, briefly describe an event that elicited a painful and intense emotional reaction. In the second column, write the perfectionist interpretation of the event and, next to it, in parentheses, the emotion that that interpretation elicited. In the third column, cognitively reconstruct the event by writing an alternative, more appropriate or rational, interpretation—the way an Optimalist would interpret the event. Next to it, in parentheses, write the emotion that you are experiencing or hope to experience alongside this interpretation. Here is an example:

| Event | Perfectionist Interpretation | Optimalist Interpretation |
|---|---|---|
| I failed an exam. | I am a loser and will never succeed. (frustration and inadequacy) | It is just one exam, and next time I will make a greater effort. (hopefulness) |
| I put on three pounds in three weeks. | I am overweight and getting more so by the day. (depression) | Being human, my weight fluctuates. I have not exercised for a month, but I will start again. (determination) |

This exercise is not a quick fix, and sometimes we need much more than cognitively reconstructing an event to shift from anxiety to hope, or from depression to determination. However, if done regularly, this exercise can significantly reduce the emotional pain associated with perfectionism and provide a healthy alternative to medication.

# Fifth Meditation: The Role of Suffering

---

Deep unspeakable suffering may well be called a baptism, a regeneration, the initiation into a new state.

—*George Eliot*

My hope, when I started on my journey to becoming an Optimalist, was to eliminate pain, sadness, anxiety, and suffering from my life. It was, of course, my perfectionism dictating my objective. I wanted to be enlightened—to find a place inside myself where I could always be content regardless of what happened outside. I did not find such a place. What I did find, however, was that there were benefits associated with suffering, and, consequently, I recognized the importance of accepting suffering.

While it is part of our universal nature to seek pleasure and avoid pain, culture plays a central role in how we deal with suffering. In the West we generally reject suffering. We see it as an unwelcome interruption of our pursuit of happiness. So we fight it, repress it, medicate it, or search for quick-fix solutions to get rid of it. In some cultures, especially in the East, suffering is acknowledged for the important role it plays in people's lives, in the meandering path toward enlightenment. While I have yet to be convinced that it is possible to reach a state of enlightenment or nirvana—a state of perfect and permanent inner peace—there is much that we can learn from the Buddhist approach to life's impermanence and imperfections, defeats and disappointments.

The Tibetan monk Khenchen Konchog Gyaltshen Rinpoche discusses four benefits of suffering: wisdom, resilience, compassion, and a deep respect for reality.[1]

Wisdom emerges from the experience of suffering. When things go well we rarely stop to ask questions about our lives and predicament. A difficult situation, however, often forces us out of our mindless state, causing us to reflect on our experiences. To be able to see deeply, to develop what King Solomon referred to as a wise heart, we must brave the eye of the storm.

Nietzsche, a wise man himself, famously remarked that what does not kill us, makes us stronger. Suffering can make us more resilient, better able to endure hardships. Just as a muscle, in order to build up, must endure some pain, so our emotions must endure pain in order to strengthen. Helen Keller, who in her lifetime knew much suffering, as well as joy, noted that "character cannot be developed in ease and quiet. Only through experience of trial and suffering can the soul be strengthened, vision cleared, ambition inspired, and success achieved."

Everybody hurts sometimes, and allowing ourselves to feel this universal emotion links us together in a web of compassion. The dictionary defines *compassion* as a "deep awareness of the suffering of another coupled with the wish to relieve it," but the only way we can gain a deep awareness of the suffering of others is by having suffered ourselves. A theoretical understanding of suffering is as meaningless as a theoretical description of the color blue to a blind person. To know it, we need to experience it. As Pastor Fritz Williams notes, "Suffering and joy teach us, if we allow them, how to make the leap of empathy, which transports us into the soul and heart of another person. In those transparent moments we know other people's joys and sorrows, and we care about their concerns as if they were our own."

One of the most significant benefits of suffering is that it breeds a deep respect for reality, for what is. While the experience of joy connects us to the realm of infinite possibilities, the experience of pain reminds us of our limitations. When, despite all our efforts, we get hurt, we are humbled by constraints that we sometimes fail to notice when we're flying high. It seems to me more than symbolic that when in ecstasy we often lift our head up, to the heavens, to the infinite, and when in agony, we tend to cast our gaze down, to earth, to the finite.

Rabbi Bunim of Pshischa says that we all need to walk around with two slips of paper in our pockets: the first slip with the Talmudic words "for my sake the world was created" and the second slip with the words from Genesis "I am but dust and ashes." The healthy psychological state resides somewhere in between the two messages, somewhere between hubris and humility. In the same way that the synthesis between hubris and humility breeds psychological health, combining ecstasy and agony establishes a healthy relationship with reality.

Ecstasy makes me feel invincible: it makes me feel that I am the master of my destiny, that I create my reality. But agony is likely to make me feel vulnerable and humbled: it makes me feel that I am the servant of my circumstances, that I have little control over my reality. Ecstasy alone leads to detached arrogance; suffering alone engenders resignation. Life's vicissitudes bring us closer to Aristotle's golden mean.

**TIME-IN** Think of a period in your life when you experienced suffering. What did you learn? In what ways did you grow?

A deep respect for reality implies an acceptance of what is—of our potential, our limitation, and our humanity. Recognizing that suffering is integral to our lives and that there are other benefits to pain, such as the cultivation of wisdom and compassion, we become more accepting of our suffering. And when we truly accept grief and sorrow as inevitable, we actually suffer less.

Nathaniel Branden refers to self-esteem—for which self-acceptance is central—as the immune system of consciousness. A strong immune system does not mean that we do not get sick but rather that we get sick less often and that when we do get sick, we recover faster. Similarly, suffering is unlikely to ever go away completely, but as the immune system of our consciousness strengthens, we suffer less often, and when we do, our recovery is more rapid.

The fact that suffering yields benefits does not imply that we ought to seek it actively—just as the fact that sickness actually strengthens our immune system does not imply that we need to look for opportunities to become sick. We naturally seek pleasure in our lives and try to minimize the amount of pain we endure. The imperfect and impermanent world provides us ample opportunities, without us actively looking for them, to fortify our immune system.

The first of the Buddha's Four Noble Truths is the truth of suffering—a truth we can either reject or accept as an inevitable part of being human. And when we learn to accept, even embrace, difficult experiences, our suffering becomes a tool, an instrument, for growth.

# EXERCISE

## Reflecting on Suffering

Take at least twenty minutes to write about a period in your life when you experienced suffering. Describe what happened, how you felt then, and what you feel now. What impact did the experience have on you? What lessons did you learn from the experience? In what ways did you grow? What else can the experience teach you? Try to write in a free-associative way without worrying about clarity or grammar.

To gain more benefit, repeat this exercise—either writing about the same experience or about another painful experience.[2]

# Sixth Meditation: The Platinum Rule

---

**Don't forget to love yourself.**

—*Søren Kierkegaard*

S ome version of the Golden Rule, reminding us to not do unto others as we would not have done unto ourselves, finds its way into most moral codes, be they secular or religious. It is with our neighbor that the Golden Rule is concerned. But what about ourselves? The Golden Rule takes the love of self for granted—the self is used as the standard for the love of others, how we treat the "I" as the standard for how we ought to treat our fellow men and women. The sages, however, generally ignored the fact that we don't all love ourselves or, rather, that many of us fall out of love with ourselves once we are old enough to turn our critical impulse, the faultfinder, inward.

We rarely condemn others for their fallibility but routinely refuse to accept our own humanity. As Diane Ackerman points out, "No one can live up to perfection, and most of us do not often expect it of others; but we are more demanding with ourselves."[1] Why the double standard, the generosity toward our neighbor and the miserliness where we ourselves are concerned? And so I propose that we add a new rule, which we can call the Platinum Rule, to our moral code: "Do not do unto yourself what you would not do unto others."

Taking as a standard our behavior toward others can help us recognize irrational, destructive attitudes toward ourselves. Would you criticize your partner if she gave a less-than-perfect speech? Would you think any less of your best friend if he did not do well on an exam? If your daughter or father did not earn first place in a competition, would their imperfect record diminish your love for them? Probably not. And yet when we ourselves fall short, we often regard ourselves as wholly inadequate, utter failures.

When the Dalai Lama and some of his followers began to work with Western scientists, they were surprised to find that self-esteem was an issue—that so many Westerners did not love themselves and that self-hate was pervasive. The discrepancy between self-love and love for others—between miserliness toward ourselves and generosity toward our neighbors—simply does not exist in Tibetan thought. In the words of the Dalai Lama, "Compassion, or *tsewa*, as it is understood in the Tibetan tradition, is a state of mind or way of being where you extend how you relate to yourself toward others as well."[2] When the Dalai Lama was then asked to clarify whether indeed the object of compassion may be the self, he responded:

Yourself first, and then in a more advanced way the aspiration will embrace others. In a way, high levels of compassion are nothing but an advanced state of that self-interest. That's why it is hard for people who have a strong sense of self-hatred to have genuine compassion toward others. There is no anchor, no basis to start from.

There is much research pointing to the importance of self-esteem when dealing with difficult experiences. Recently, however, psychologists Mark Leary and his colleagues have illustrated that especially in hard times, compassion toward the self is actually more helpful than self-esteem is.[3] Leary explains, "Self-compassion helps people not to add a layer of self-recrimination on top of whatever bad things happen to them. If people learn only to feel better about themselves but continue to beat themselves up when they fail or make mistakes, they will be unable to cope nondefensively with their difficulties."

Self-compassion includes being understanding and kind toward oneself, mindfully accepting painful thoughts and feelings, and recognizing that one's difficult experiences are part of being human. It is also about being forgiving toward ourselves if we perform poorly on an exam, make a mistake at work, or get upset when we shouldn't. Leary notes that "American society has spent a great deal of time and effort trying to promote people's self-esteem when a far more important ingredient of well-being may be self-compassion."

While Leary's emphasis on self-compassion is important, the distinction he and others make between self-compassion and self-esteem may be unnecessary. Nathaniel Branden highlights self-acceptance, which is very similar to Leary's self-compassion, as one of the pillars of self-esteem. Self-compassion and self-esteem are inextricably linked.

**TIME-IN** Are you compassionate toward yourself? Could you be more compassionate?

When altruism—selflessness, the negation of the self—was put on a pedestal as the Western world's moral ideal, self-love became the enemy, and every attempt possible has been made to root it out. This assault on human nature—on self-love and its corollary self-interest—has led to horrific consequences, both politically (in communist societies, for example) and individually (with the low self-esteem epidemic).

The call for altruism has taken the Golden Rule and distorted it, taking the part on loving others out of context, away from its emotional root, which is self-love. Trying to decrease self-love as a way to increase love toward others leads to the opposite outcome. Loving others presupposes loving oneself, or as the philosopher and author Ayn Rand puts it, "To say 'I love you' one must first be able to say the 'I.'"

# EXERCISE

## .*●Sentence Completion

Complete the following sentence stems. Remember to do them first without thinking too much and only afterward to analyze the responses that you generated.

If I love myself 5 percent more . . .

To increase my self-esteem . . .

To become 5 percent more compassionate toward myself . . .

To become 5 percent more compassionate toward others . . .

I am beginning to see that . . .

14

# Seventh Meditation: Yes, but . . .

The important work of moving the world
forward does not wait to be done by perfect men.

—*George Eliot*

attended a dinner party last week. The conversation mean-
dered from affairs of the heart to current political affairs, from
food and cooking to sports and literature. At a certain point
we went around the table and talked about books that have influ-
enced us. When my turn came, I talked passionately about *Built
to Last*, which discusses visionary companies—organizations that
had a significant impact on our world through their strong values
and strong culture. When I mentioned Walt Disney as an exem-
plar of a visionary leader who made a considerable contribution to
society, I was interrupted by the hostess: "Yes, but I heard that he
was mean to his employees." The "yes, but" gavel strikes again.

When people talk about Bill Gates, they may mention his technological contribution or his brilliant business skills, and then,
almost always, the gavel strikes: "Yes, but he thwarted competition." Yes, John Piermont Morgan helped the U.S. government on

a number of occasions and set high standards for doing business, but he engaged in some shady deals. Great political figures are not spared the "yes, but" treatment. Yes, Lincoln freed the slaves, but in a speech in Charleston before the American Civil War, he advocated the superiority of the white race. And yes, Gandhi may have led India to freedom, but he was at times cruel to his wife. The list goes on.

Lincoln's personal indifference to slavery (if true) is, to say the least, disappointing, but his actions led millions of people from slavery to freedom. J. P. Morgan may not have been a saint, but he nevertheless played an important role in developing confidence and trust in the economy and made the United States the most prosperous country in the world. And yet people dismiss these heroic figures with an offhand remark, unwilling to accept that a hero, outside storybooks and fairy tales, is, first and foremost, a human being. The question is not whether the perfect hero exists but whether we choose to focus on the core characteristics of the person, on his achievements and contributions, or actively seek (and inevitably find) a fault.

Whether we choose to focus on the positive or negative determines what we see in others and in ourselves. A person who focuses on the negative—the faultfinding Perfectionist—sees the bad as the active force in the world and the good as the passive force, the absence of the bad. A person with a positive view—the benefit-finding Optimist—perceives the good as the generative force in reality and the bad as the absence of good.

It is no coincidence that the metaphysics of most religions and belief systems, describe the good as light and the bad as darkness. Light is an active force; darkness, the absence of light, is passive. A dark patch does not bring darkness to a lit-up room, as a single candle lights up a dark space. When Edmund Burke said that "all it takes for evil to triumph is for good men to do nothing," he recognized the proper relationship between the positive and negative forces in reality: evil is the absence of good.

The implications of a negative focus—the belief that good can exist only if bad is completely absent—is that only a person without any dark patches, without any blemishes, can be good. No person can pass this test, and therefore no person can be worthy of our admiration.

The implications of a positive focus—the belief that the bad is passive and the good is active—is that our world can only be made better by people who *do* good, by courageous people who *act*. By virtue of acting in this world, these people also inevitably make mistakes, but this is the risk they take and the price they pay.

Beyond determining how we evaluate others, our approach—whether we focus on the positive or the negative—has a direct impact on the way we lead our lives. What we focus on determines whether we lead an active or a passive life. Do we spend our lives running away from unhappiness (negative) or pursuing happiness (positive)? Do we passively avoid depression or actively seek joy? Do we spend most of our time generating light or spend our days avoiding darkness? Do we lead an active albeit risky life (promoting the good) or play it safe and do nothing (avoiding the bad)? A negative focus leads to fear as the primary driving force—fear of making mistakes, fear of imperfection, fear of castigation. After all, no one, not even our cultural icons, is able to remain pure in our own eyes or the eyes of others, so who are we to try and why should we even bother?

Perfectionists who focus on the negative are so afraid of doing something wrong that they often refrain from action, conform to the status quo, and end up doing nothing. In contrast, Optimalists who focus on the positive understand that to act is, at times, to err but that it's not the avoidance of making mistakes that creates the good life but rather the active pursuit of the good. Focusing on the good does not mean ignoring the bad but rather the understanding that the most effective way to eradicate the bad is to do good.

**TIME-IN** Consider where you may be using the "yes, but" gavel, either in your relation to cultural icons or in your intimate relationships. What price do you pay for this form of dismissal?

In history—whether our own, our heroes', or the world's—we will always find dark patches, damned spots that taint purity. How we choose to deal with these flaws will determine our personal and collective futures. Do we shut ourselves in a barrel out of fear that we might taint our hands even more, or do we follow the risky path of Prometheus, who gave fire to mortals and risked being burned? Do we remain passive socialites who disapprove, or do we become social activists who improve?

To criticize great men and women for their wrongdoings, for their errors, is easy—for no person is perfect. But as Theodore Roosevelt said in 1910:

> It is not the critic who counts, not the man who points
> out how the strong man stumbled, or where the doer of
> deeds could have done better. The credit belongs to the
> man who is actually in the arena; whose face is marred
> by the dust and sweat and blood; who strives valiantly;
> who errs and comes short again and again, because there
> is no effort without error or shortcoming; who knows
> the great enthusiasms, the great devotions and spends
> himself for a worthy cause; who, at the best, knows in
> the end the triumph of high achievement, and who,
> at the worst, if he fails, at least he fails while daring

greatly; so that his place shall never be with those cold
and timid souls who knew neither victory or defeat.

To do no harm by not doing makes one a coward, not a saint.
The true heroes are those who permit themselves to be human—
who understand that to do good is to risk failure, that to act is
to risk getting dirty. And we, who sit around the dinner table,
should say grace and thank those brave, imperfect mortals.

## EXERCISE

### ●●● Making a Difference

What can you do to make the world a better place? Commit to one
or two activities that would, in some way, contribute to others—
whether writing an op-ed to your local paper about a personally
meaningful topic, volunteering in your children's school, or spending extra time with a friend in need. Don't wait. Just do it, even if you
do it imperfectly.

When you give, you receive. There are numerous benefits to
prosocial behavior, from increased well-being to improved physical
health.[1]

# 15

# Eighth Meditation: The Pro-Aging Industry

---

**How pleasant is the day when we give up striving to be young—or slender.**

—*William James*

In a study of elderly men and women, Becca Levy of Yale University School of Public Health found that people's perceptions of aging significantly affected their longevity. Those with a positive view of old age lived on average more than seven years longer than those with a negative view.[1] Levy's research also demonstrated that a positive perception of old age affects the quality of life, leading those who accepted old age and the aging process to enjoy significantly higher levels of physical and mental health. One of Levy's studies showed that activating positive stereotypes of aging (such as wisdom) improved elderly people's memory, while activating negative stereotypes (such as senility) worsened their memory. Beliefs become self-fulfilling prophecies.

Cultures vary in their perceptions of old age; these perceptions, in turn, affect the beliefs of individuals within that culture and, consequently, their mental and physical health. American culture, for example, takes a generally negative view of aging, and Americans suffer significantly more memory loss in old age than Asians, who by and large come from cultures where getting older is looked upon favorably. It is easier, it seems, to become a Chinese sage than an American one.

Our beliefs about aging can also affect us when we're young. If we perceive aging as something to be avoided, then we are likely to spend more time trying to escape the fate that awaits us. If, on the other hand, we appreciate and value old age, then we have much to look forward to and pursue. We enjoy greater mental and physical health when we spend our time pursuing a positive instead of avoiding a negative, especially when it is something as inescapable as age.

In America and other anti-aging cultures, millions of people take extreme measures—spending inordinate amounts of time, energy, and money—to reverse nature's course. While there is nothing inherently wrong with trying to look younger and a lot that is right with maintaining our physical fitness throughout our lives, there is everything wrong with refusing to accept and obsessively fighting the natural process of aging.

To lead happier, healthier, and longer lives, we need to change our perception of aging by accepting reality for what it is. Whether we like it or not, we change over time, in some aspects for the better, in others for the worse. We are all well aware of the downside, especially the physical downside, of aging. But what we focus on less is that aging provides us with tremendous intellectual, emotional, and spiritual opportunities for growth.

My intention is not to romanticize old age but simply to make it real, both the good and the bad. It is, of course, true that growing old, at times, can bring about difficulties, such as ill health, impacting the elderly person in unexpected and unwanted ways.

But it is equally true that there are potential benefits that come with age. What we are able to see and understand, know and appreciate, when we're sixty or eighty is different from what we are capable of when we are twenty or thirty. There are no shortcuts to mental and emotional maturity; wisdom, judiciousness, intelligence, and perspective potentially develop with time and experience. Healthy aging is about actively accepting the real challenges that come with age, while appreciating the real opportunities that arise as we grow older.

For those with negative perceptions of old age, life becomes a battle against losing their youth, a battle they cannot win; the outcome is inevitably frustration and unhappiness—not just when they become old but when they are still young. In contrast, those who appreciate old age can derive much benefit from the natural process of aging and growing. In the words of Oliver Wendell Holmes, "To be seventy years young is sometimes far more cheerful and hopeful than to be forty years old."

**TIME-IN** In what ways have you developed and improved over time, with age? How do you hope to continue to do so?

One of the reasons for the negative perception that some have toward aging is that, by and large, the younger generation today no longer looks to the older generation for advice; consequently, the young, and sometimes the elderly themselves, fail to see and appreciate the wisdom that can come with age. Technology, at least in part, is to blame. Today, because technological knowledge becomes obsolete before the ink dries, the order of nature has been reversed and the young are teaching the old. Generalizing from "technological knowledge" to "all knowledge," many young people, believing that they have all the answers, do not respect the wisdom of their elders or appreciate the value of life experience.

An important part of cultivating an independent sense of self, a process that usually begins during the teenage years, is dismissing the wisdom of the older generation, enjoying that feeling of invincibility and the desire to live life on one's own terms. While this may be natural and right for a teenager, a mature adult learns to learn from others, especially those who have more experience. Mark Twain famously captured this natural process from dismissal to appreciation: "When I was a boy of fourteen, my father was so ignorant I could hardly stand to have the old man around. But when I got to be twenty-one, I was astonished at how much the old man had learned in seven years."

In the Bible we are commanded to "honor thy father and thy mother: that thy days may be long upon the land which the Lord thy God giveth thee." Today we have scientific evidence that illustrates the connection that the Bible makes, between honoring our parents, or the elderly in general, and longevity. When we honor and respect the wisdom of older people—be they our parents or others—when we spend time listening to them and learning from them, we become more appreciative of them and, by extension, of aging. And as the research shows, a positive view of old age makes us live longer—as well as better.

On the societal level, we would do well to divert some of the funds currently being invested in the anti-aging industry toward the creation, or improvement, of a pro-aging industry.[2] This would mean, for instance, that we would be better off diverting money from cosmetics and plastic surgery to educational programs for lifelong learning.

Oscar Wilde once commented that "youth is wasted on the young"; in the case of those who do not appreciate the benefits of growing older, we can say that age is wasted on the elderly.

Whether we are twenty or eighty, the choice between spending the rest of our life fighting nature's course or embracing it is ours to make—right now.

# EXERCISE

## Learning from Elders

Engage in conversations with people who are older than you or who have more experience than you have in one area or another. What can you learn from them? Ask them about their life experiences— their mistakes and their triumphs—and what they have learned from those. Listen—really listen—to what they have to say.

While I certainly do not advocate putting our critical faculty aside as we absorb the advice of other people, young or old, I certainly do advocate being open to the wisdom that can only come with experience. Not only will we learn a great deal about our life, but we are also more likely to appreciate the elderly and thus cultivate a more positive view of old age.

# Ninth Meditation: The Great Deception

We sense that we are impostors. Keeping our feelings a secret, we assume no one on earth is as neurotic, no one as uniquely flawed.

—*Diane Ackerman*

There has been much change, and some progress, since the nineteenth century and the reign of Queen Victoria. Revolutions, like tidal waves, created a new world order, not just politically but in our everyday mores—in the way we dress and talk, in the way we approach sex and art. The shift over the past century or two, broadly speaking, has been from excessive prudishness to what many might argue is excessive openness. On closer scrutiny, though, we see that much of this change seems more significant than it actually is.

We pride ourselves on having become less restrained and inhibited than our ancestors, but progress has only been skin deep, at best. While we have learned to expose our bodies, our hearts remain buried, and while discourse of rough sex is permitted, talk of tender love is taboo. New York streets may sizzle with bare flesh in summer, but we bare our souls only in the privacy of the therapist's office. We have become—or, perhaps, have remained—emotional prudes.

In nineteenth-century England, New England, and beyond, the mark of a true lady was her ability to mask her feelings and suppress her desires; the mark of a true gentleman was his ability to transcend his emotions. Today many of us—and perfectionists in particular—feel that we must suppress our emotional discomfort and be—or at the very least *seem*—happy.

This perfectionist expectation, to display an unbroken chain of positive emotions, leads to much unhappiness. We are taught to hide our pain, fake a smile, put on a brave face. And when most of what we see are perfect smiles displayed on other people's perfectly tanned faces, we begin to believe that we are the odd ones out—because we are sometimes sad or lonely or we don't feel as happy or as put together as everyone else appears to be. Not wanting to be the odd one out, to ruin the festive circus and reveal our shameful feelings, we hide our unhappiness with our own clown mask, and when asked how we are, we respond, with a wink and a smile, "Just great." And then we run to the psychiatrist's office and command her, though she needs no commanding, to make our sadness go away. We join the march of folly, become accomplices in the great deception that denies humanity's humanity.

In his book *Radical Honesty*, Brad Blanton writes, "We all lie like hell. It wears us out. It is the major source of all human stress. Lying kills people."[1] For most people (the psychopath being an exception), lying is stressful, which is why lie detectors generally work. When we hide part of ourselves, when we lie about how we feel, the normal stress associated with lying is compounded by the stress of suppressing emotions. Conversely, when we acknowledge how we feel, to ourselves and to those close to us, we are more likely to experience the calm that comes with honesty, the release and relief that come with giving ourselves the permission to be human.

In a recent report published in Germany, people who have to smile for a living (such as sales assistants and flight attendants) were found to be more prone to depression, stress, cardiovascular problems, and high blood pressure.[2] Most people need to put on a mask for at least part of the day; basic human courtesy requires that we sometimes curb our emotions, whether they be anger or frustration or passion. The solution to this problem—whether one is required to pretend for much of the day working in the service industry or for only some of the day, as anyone interacting with other people has to do—is to find what Brian Little calls a "restorative niche." The niche can include sharing our feelings with a trusted friend, writing whatever comes to mind in a personal journal, or simply spending time alone in our room. Depending on our constitution, some of us may need ten minutes to recover from the emotional deception, and others may need hours. The key during the recovery period is to do away with pretense, to be real, and to allow ourselves to feel any emotion that arises.

Much has been written and said about positive self-talk—for example, repeating to ourselves "I am wonderful" when we feel down, "I am strong" when going through a rough patch, or "I am getting better every day in every way" each morning in front of the mirror. The evidence that this sort of pep talk works is weak, and there are psychologists who suggest that it can actually hurt more than it can help. Little, unfortunately, has been written about *real self-talk*, acknowledging honestly what we are feeling at a given point. When feeling down, saying "I am really sad" or "I feel so torn"—to ourselves or to someone we trust—is much more helpful than declaring "I am tough" or "I am happy."

**TIME-IN** Where in your life are you required to put on an emotional mask? Where and with whom in your life can you create restorative niches?

Not only do we make ourselves unhappy when we suppress emotions, when we pretend, but we make others unhappy as well. In this way, the great deception (pretending that we are really happy when we are not) contributes to the great depression (to the rising levels of unhappiness in the world). In putting on the facade, we communicate to others that everyone is doing just great, except for them, which makes them feel worse and even more determined to hide their pain. By perpetually hiding our emotions, we don't give others permission to share their own. And in turn, their brave faces communicate to us that everyone else is doing great, and we consequently feel even worse. And so we all continue, smiling our way through the insincere dance of words and gestures, engaged in a downward spiral of deception and depression.

There are those who believe that the common tendency to feel better when others reveal their pain exposes our dark side. The Germans have a word for it, *Schadenfreude*, which Gary Coleman of *Avenue Q* defines as "happiness at the misfortune of others." But there is another, more generous interpretation of why others' sharing of their pain can lead to our gain: we feel better because we recognize that we are normal and we are not alone.

The call for more emotional openness is not a call to wear our hearts on our sleeves, which is not always fitting or helpful. But there is a healthy middle-ground between full disclosure and total concealment. An occasional honest answer, like "a bit sad" or "slightly anxious," in response to a *genuine* "How are you?" can help us, and those around us, feel a little less sad and slightly more hopeful. While we should leave full disclosures to pillow talk, the therapist's couch, or our password-protected computer screen, we would do well to restrict the use of our perfect mask, perhaps wearing it to a stuffy board meeting or a Halloween party.

There are those who argue that, emotionally speaking, we have actually regressed since the Victorian era. Psychiatrist Julius Heuscher, lamenting the modern disparagement of revealing emotions, quotes the legendary French entertainer Maurice Chevalier: "Girls used to blush when they were ashamed, now they are ashamed when they blush." So rather than pretending to have made progress, as we do when passing judgment on Victorian mores, we need to make real progress—and that requires being real.

# EXERCISE

## ●● Sentence Completion

Generate at least six endings to each of the following sentence stems, as quickly as you can, without analyzing or thinking too much. After you have completed them, look at your responses, reflect on them, and, in writing, commit to action.

To be 5 percent more open about my feelings . . .
If I am more open about my feelings . . .
If I bring 5 percent more awareness to my fears . . .
When I hide my emotions . . .
To become 5 percent more real . . .

# Tenth Meditation: Knowing and Not Knowing

---

**The invariable mark of wisdom is to see the miraculous in the common.**

*—Ralph Waldo Emerson*

We fear the unknown. We desperately want to know what happened last summer, or last night, or in prehistoric times. We want to know what will happen next week and what the world will look like ten or a thousand years from now. We seek certainty in the present, to know what our life is really about right now. More than bad news, we fear no news; an uncertain diagnosis often feels worse to us than a certain, albeit negative, one. Beyond mere curiosity, our desire to know is a deep existential need—for if knowledge is power, then its absence implies weakness.

The discovery—or, as some would argue, the invention—of God alleviates the anxiety that comes with not knowing. Mortals who promise certainty are crowned kings. When our future is threatened, as in times of war, we follow the leader who promises us the comfort of definitive knowledge. When we are sick, we put the doctor on a pedestal. As children, we look to seemingly omniscient adults to reduce our anxiety. Later, once our parents' imperfections are revealed, they are replaced by God, guru, or guide.

And yet deep down we experience anxiety, because deep down we know that we do not know. History, archaeology, and psychology cannot fully explain our collective and private pasts. Vivid descriptions of the afterlife, next month's horoscope, and, alas, even fortune cookies do not provide us with a clear picture of what tomorrow, or the day after, will bring. And when we really think about it, we have no clue even as to what the present is all about.

How do we overcome this fear? Religion certainly helps, which explains why believers are generally happier than nonbelievers. Belonging to a group that has clear rules and boundaries can also bring some clarity to our confusion. Reading the *New England Journal of Medicine*, *Psychological Bulletin*, the *European Journal of Archaeology*, or the latest issue of *Science Magazine* can help us sleep better at night, for while these scholarly journals may not have all the answers, they surely have some of them. But usually, ultimately, these are not enough.

So what can we do? We need to accept that we sometimes do not and cannot know. We need to embrace uncertainty in order to feel more comfortable in its presence. Then, once we feel comfortable with our ignorance, we are better prepared to reconstruct our discomfort with the unknown into a sense of awe and wonder. It is about relearning to perceive the world—and our lives—as a miracle unfolding.

The word *miracle* stems from *mirus*, Latin for "wonder." Miracles, if taken to denote an event "that excites admiring and awe," do not just happen in fairy tales, to past generations, to saints—in the supernatural realm. Nature itself, in its entirety, is a miracle. As Ralph Waldo Emerson reminds us, "If the stars should appear one night in a thousand years, how would men believe and adore; and preserve for many generations the remembrance of the city of God which had been shown! But every night come out these envoys of beauty, and light the universe with their admonishing smile."

The stars, the trees, the animals are, in fact, a mystifying phenomenon, a miracle. The fact that we write, that we see, that we feel and think—that we *are*—is a miracle. The thread of time that links past, present, and future is inexplicable, a miracle. In the words of George Bernard Shaw, "Miracles, in the sense of phenomena we cannot explain, surround us on every hand: life itself is the miracle of miracles."

There is nothing defeatist about accepting, and embracing, our own and others' not knowing. In his essay "Leadership as the Legitimation of Doubt," organizational behaviorist Karl Weick argues that the most successful people embrace uncertainty and are not afraid to admit that they don't know.[1]

Healthy acceptance of uncertainty is not, quite, to go as far as Socrates did when he declared that he was the wisest man alive "for I know one thing, and that is that I know nothing." There are, of course, things that we know with a high degree of certainty, for while the stars are awe inspiring, we know that they will shine again once day turns to night; while we do not really know why, we do know that trees will continue to grow given sunlight, water, and air; and while I have no control over my mortality, I know that right now I am alive—that the present certainly is, and in the here-and-now I know that I think, and I know that I am.

The healthy approach to take toward our pervasive, yet selective, ignorance is a realistic one—one that embraces our not knowing as it does our knowing. We need to accept the things we cannot know as well as the things we can. Then, the next time we face a fork in the road—which is right now and at every other moment in our life—rather than approaching it with fear over not fully knowing what lies ahead or behind or right in front of us, we can learn to approach it with awe. We are, after all, living miracles.

# EXERCISE

## Just Walk

The late Phil Stone, one of the pioneers of positive psychology, was much more than my teacher. Beyond sharing his vast knowledge of the social sciences with me, he was extremely generous with his time when it came to counseling and supporting me. He is my role model for the kind of teacher I try to be to my students.

In 1999 Phil took me with him to Lincoln, Nebraska, to attend the first-ever Positive Psychology Summit. The second day of the conference was a clichéd September day—the sky was partly cloudy, the breeze warm and pleasant. After the morning lectures Phil said to me, "Let's go for a walk."

"Walk where?" I asked.

"Just walk."

It was one of the most important lessons I had ever learned.

Go for a walk outside, without a specific agenda other than to slow down—to experience and savor and appreciate the richness of our world. Simply take your time, as you sense the pulse of the city, the calm of a village, the expansiveness of the ocean, or the richness of the woods. Make *just walking* a regular ritual.

Helen Keller tells a story about a friend who had just returned from a long walk in the woods. When Keller asked her friend what she had observed, the friend replied, "Nothing in particular." Keller writes:

I wondered how it was possible to walk for an hour through the woods and see nothing of note. I who cannot see find hundreds of things: the delicate symmetry of a leaf, the smooth skin of a silver birch, the rough, shaggy bark of a pine. I who am blind can give one hint to those who see: use your eyes as if tomorrow you will have been stricken blind. Hear the music of voices, the songs of a bird, the mighty strains of an orchestra as if you would be stricken deaf tomorrow. Touch each object as if tomorrow your tactile sense would fail. Smell the perfume of flowers, taste with relish each morsel, as if tomorrow you could never taste or smell again. Make the most of every sense. Glory in all the facets and pleasures and beauty which the world reveals to you.

# Conclusion

> God, grant me the serenity to accept the things
> I cannot change, the courage to change the
> things I can change, and the wisdom to know
> the difference.
>
> —*Reinhold Niebuhr*

My name is Tal, and I am a Perfectionist.

Accepting that perfectionism will always be part of my life has been liberating. Paradoxically, recognizing that perfectionism never goes away completely makes me more of an Optimalist.

There is no moment in life—as, in the past, I had hoped there would be—when we switch from perfectionism to optimalism, when we cease to reject failure and painful emotions and, at times, success. We do, however, have the potential to increase the number of moments when we accept that we have fallen short, when we embrace our hurt feelings, and when we allow ourselves to appreciate and enjoy our accomplishments.

Perfectionism and optimalism are not distinct ways of being, an either-or choice, but rather they coexist in each person. And while we can move from perfectionism toward optimalism, we never fully leave perfectionism behind and never fully reach optimalism ahead. The optimalism ideal is not a distant shore to be reached but a distant star that guides us and can never be reached. As Carl Rogers pointed out, "The good life is a process, not a state of being. It is a direction, not a destination."[1]

Almost two decades have passed since I first resolved to deal with my perfectionism, and the struggle continues. However, the struggle is not a Sisyphean one. There has been real progress, and the quality of the struggle has changed over the years. Today I enjoy more of the journey and I accept—sometimes even marvel at—the downs and the ups. Perfectionism is a part of me, and so is optimalism. And today, I can say, without violating Aristotle's law of noncontradiction:

My name is Tal, and I am *also* an Optimalist.

# Notes

Complete bibliographical information can be found in the References section.

**Introduction**
1. Reported in Blatt (1995).
2. Burns (1980).
3. Hamachek (1978).
4. I draw on the work of Hewitt and Flett (1991), as well as Frost et al. (1990), who describe perfectionism as a multidimensional construct.
5. This definition is taken from *The Positive Psychology Manifesto*, which was first introduced by some of the leading researchers in the field in 1999. The full definition: "Positive Psychology is the scientific study of optimal human functioning. It aims to discover and promote the factors that allow individuals and communities to thrive. The positive psychology movement represents a new commitment on the part of research psychologists to focus attention upon the sources of psychological health, thereby going beyond prior emphases upon disease and disorder."
6. Rogers (1961).

**Chapter 1**
1. Frost et al. (1990) discuss "concern over mistakes" as one of the dimensions of perfectionism.
2. Carson and Langer (2006).

3. Pacht (1984). Burns (1999) extensively discusses the all-or-nothing approach.
4. The relativist, in fact, is a Perfectionist in disguise, subscribing to the notion that there are absolutely no absolutes.
5. See Morling and Epstein (1997), as well as Swann et al. (1989).
6. Thoreau (2004).
7. Emerson (1983).
8. Frost et al. (1990), Flett et al. (1992), Flett and Hewitt (2002), Franco-Paredes et al. (2005), and Bardone-Cone et al. (2007).
9. Branden (1994).
10. Bednar and Peterson (1995).
11. Blatt (1995).
12. Bardone-Cone et al. (2007).
13. Rogers (1961).
14. Reported in Bardone-Cone et al. (2007).
15. Yerkes and Dodson (1908).
16. Gardner (1994).
17. Flett et al. (1992).
18. Koch (2005) and Mancini (2007).
19. Bem (1967).
20. Carson and Langer (2006).
21. For more on the benefits of keeping a journal, see Pennebaker (1997).

## Chapter 2

1. See Wegner (1994) and Wenzlaff and Wegner (2000).
2. See Barlow and Craske (2006) and Craske et al. (2004).
3. Ricard (2006).
4. Williams et al. (2007).
5. Williams et al. (2007).
6. See Lyubomirsky (2007) and Ray et al. (2008).
7. Pennebaker (1997).
8. Branden (1994).
9. Kabat-Zinn (1990).
10. Rogers (1961).
11. Newman et al. (1997).
12. Calhoun and Tedeschi (2005).
13. Kuhn (1996).
14. Gibran (1923).

15. See Maslow (1993) and James (1988).
16. Worden (2008).
17. Emerson (1983).
18. Kabat-Zinn (1990).
19. Bennett-Goleman (2002).

## Chapter 3
1. Camus (1991).
2. Ackerman (1995).
3. James (1890).
4. Csikszentmihalyi (1998).
5. Locke and Latham (2002).
6. Collins (2001).
7. Hackman (2002).
8. Domar and Kelly (2008).
9. Nash and Stevenson (2005).
10. Reivich and Shatte (2003).
11. See Cooperrider and Whitney (2005).
12. See Emmons and McCullough (2003) and Emmons (2007).
13. Lyubomirsky (2007).
14. Kosslyn (2005).
15. Langer (1989).
16. Seligman et al. (2005).

## Chapter 4
1. Ackerman (1995).
2. Sowell (2007).
3. Pinker (2006).
4. Branden (1994).
5. Ginott (2003).
6. I recommend doing a longer sentence-completion program, such as the one found in Nathaniel Branden's (1994) book *The Six Pillars of Self-Esteem*. An extensive program is also available online: nathanielbranden.com/catalog/articles_essays/sentence _completion.html.
7. Langer (1989).

## Chapter 5
1. Luthar et al. (2006).
2. Siegle and Schuler (2000).

3. Montessori (1995).
4. Rathunde and Csikszentmihalyi (2005a, b).
5. Winnicott (1982) and Winnicott (1990).
6. Smiles (1958).
7. Dweck (2005).
8. Dewey (2007).
9. Dewey (1997).
10. Collins (1990) and Collins (1992).

## Chapter 6

1. Edmondson (1999).
2. Mark Cannon and Amy Edmondson (2005) coauthored a paper titled "Failing to Learn and Learning to Fail (Intelligently): How Great Organizations Put Failure to Work to Innovate and Improve."
3. Edgar Scheine and Warren Bennis (1965) first introduced the term *psychological safety*. Edmondson extended their idea beyond the individual level to *team psychological safety*.
4. Cited in Cannon and Edmondson (2005).
5. Goleman et al. (2002).
6. McEvoy and Beatty (1989).
7. Cannon and Edmondson (2005).
8. Hurley and Ryman (2008).
9. Loehr and Schwartz (2001) and Loehr and Schwartz (2004).

## Chapter 7

1. The quote is attributed to Leo Buscaglia, a professor at the University of Southern California who was a popular speaker and writer. While Buscaglia's work in the area of human potential is extremely important and valuable, this particular passage is potentially damaging.
2. Gottman (2000).
3. Schnarch (1998).
4. Mill (1974).
5. Emerson (1983).
6. Burke (1898).

## Chapter 8

1. Langer (1989).
2. Nir (2008).

## Chapter 9
1. Tomaka et al. (1997).
2. Carlson (1996).

## Chapter 10
1. Rogers (1961).

## Chapter 11
1. Wilson (2008).

## Chapter 12
1. Gyaltshen Rinpoche (2006).
2. Pennebaker (1997).

## Chapter 13
1. Ackerman (1995).
2. Davidson and Harrington (2001).
3. Leary et al. (2007).

## Chapter 14
1. Lyubomirsky (2007).

## Chapter 15
1. Levy (2003) and Levy et al. (2002).
2. Dove, manufacturer of personal care products, has come up with a very successful pro-aging campaign challenging the anti-aging movement.

## Chapter 16
1. Blanton (2005).
2. dw-world.de/dw/article/0,2144,3333396,00.html. Retrieved October 13, 2008.

## Chapter 17
1. Weick (2001).

## Conclusion
1. Rogers (1961).

# References

Ackerman, D. (1995). *A Natural History of Love.* Vintage.

Bandura, A. (1997). *Self-Efficacy: The Exercise of Control.* W. H. Freeman and Company.

Bardone-Cone, A. M., Wonderlich, S. A., Frost, R. O., Bulik C. M., Mitchell, J. E., Uppala, S., and Simonich, H. (2007). Perfectionism and Eating Disorders: Current Status and Future Directions. *Clinical Psychology Review, 27,* 384–405.

Barlow, D. H., and Craske, M. G. (2006). *Mastery of Your Anxiety and Panic: Workbook.* Oxford University Press.

Bednar, R. L., and Peterson, S. R. (1995). *Self Esteem: Paradoxes and Innovations in Clinical Theory and Practice.* American Psychological Association.

Bem, D. J. (1967). Self-Perception: An Alternative Interpretation of Cognitive Dissonance Phenomena. *Psychological Review, 74,* 183–200.

Bem, D. J. (1996). Exotic Becomes Erotic: A Developmental Theory of Sexual Orientation. *Psychological Review,* 103, 320–335.

Ben-Shahar, T. (2007). *Happier: Learn the Secrets to Daily Joy and Lasting Fulfillment.* McGraw-Hill.

Bennett-Goleman, T. (2002). *Emotional Alchemy: How the Mind Can Heal the Heart.* Three Rivers Press.

Blanton, B. (2005). *Radical Honesty: How to Transform Your Life by Telling the Truth.* SparrowHawk.

Blatt, S. J. (1995). The Destructiveness of Perfectionism: Implications for the Treatment of Depression. *American Psychologist,* 50(12), 1003–1020.

Branden, N. (1994). *The Six Pillars of Self-Esteem*. Bantam Books.

Burns, D. (1980, November). The Perfectionist's Script for Self Defeat. *Psychology Today*, 34–57.

Burns, D. (1999). *Feeling Good: The New Mood Therapy*. Harper.

Burke, E. (1898). *Reflections on the Revolution in France*. MacMillan Company.

Calhoun, L. G., and Tedeschi, R. G. (2005). *The Handbook of Posttraumatic Growth: Research and Practice*. Lawrence Erlbaum Associates.

Camus, A. (1991). *The Myth of Sisyphus and Other Essays*. Vintage.

Cannon, M. D., and Edmondson, A. C. (2005). Failing to Learn and Learning to Fail (Intelligently): How Great Organizations Put Failure to Work to Innovate and Improve. *Long Range Planning*, 38, 299–319.

Carlson, R. (1996). *Don't Sweat the Small Stuff . . . and It's All Small Stuff*. Hyperion.

Carson, S. H., and Langer, E. J. (2006). Mindfulness and Self Acceptance. *Journal of Rational-Emotive and Cognitive-Behavior Therapy*, 24, 29–43.

Cavafy, C. P. (1992). *Collected Poems*. Translated by Edmund Keeley and Philip Sherrard. Edited by George Savidis. Princeton University Press.

Collins, J. (2001). *Good to Great: Why Some Companies Make the Leap . . . and Others Don't*. Collins Business.

Collins, M. (1990). *The Marva Collins' Way*. Tarcher.

Collins, M. (1992). *Ordinary Children, Extraordinary Teachers*. Hampton Roads.

Cooperrider, D. L., and Whitney, D. (2005). *Appreciative Inquiry: A Positive Revolution in Change*. Berrett-Koehler Publishers.

Craske, M. G., Barlow, D. H., and O'Leary, T. L. (2004). *Mastery of Your Anxiety and Panic: Client Workbook*. Oxford University Press.

Csikszentmihalyi, M. (1998). *Finding Flow: The Psychology of Engagement with Everyday Life*. Basic Books.

Davidson, R. J., and Harrington, A. (2001). *Visions of Compassion: Western Scientists and Tibetan Buddhists Examine Human Nature*. Oxford University Press.

Dawes, R. M. (1996). *House of Cards: Psychology and Psychotherapy Built on Myth*. Free Press.

Dewey, J. (1997). *Experience and Education*. Free Press.

Dewey, J. (2007). *Democracy and Education*. Echo Library.

Domar, A., and Kelly, A. L. (2008). *Be Happy Without Being Perfect: How to Break Free from the Perfection Deception*. Crown.

Dweck, C. S. (2005). *Mind-set: The New Psychology of Success*. Ballantine Books.

Edmondson, A. (1999). Psychological Safety and Learning Behavior in Work Teams. *Administrative Science Quarterly*, 44, 350–383.

Emerson, R. W. (1983). *Emerson: Essays and Lectures*. Library of America.

Emmons, R. A. (2007). *Thanks! How the New Science of Gratitude Can Make You Happier*. Houghton Mifflin.

Emmons, R. A., and McCullough, M. E. (2003). Counting Blessings Versus Burdens: An Experimental Investigation of Gratitude and Subjective Well-Being in Daily Life. *Journal of Personality and Social Psychology*, 88, 377–389.

Flett, G. L., Blankstein, K. R., Hewitt, P. L., and Koledin, S. (1992). Components of Perfectionism and Procrastination in College Students. *Social Behavior and Personality*, 20, 85–94.

Flett, G. L., and Hewitt, P. L. (2002). *Perfectionism: Theory, Research, and Treatment*. American Psychological Association.

Franco-Paredes, K., Mancilla-Diaz, J. M., Vazquez-Arevalo, R., Lopez-Aguilar, X., and Alvarez-Rayon, G. (2005). Perfectionism and Eating Disorders: A Review of the Literature. *European Eating Disorders Review*, 13, 61–70.

Frost, R. O., Marten, P., Lahart, C., and Rosenblate, R. (1990). The Dimensions of Perfectionism. *Cognitive Therapy and Research*, 14, 449–468.

Gardner, H. (1994). *Creating Minds: An Anatomy of Creativity as Seen Through the Lives of Freud, Einstein, Picasso, Stravinsky, Eliot, Graham, and Gandhi*. Basic Books.

Gibran, K. (1923). *The Prophet*. Knopf.

Ginott, H. G. (1995). *Teacher and Child: A Book for Parents and Teachers*. Collier Books.

Ginott, H. G. (2003). *Between Parent and Child*. Three Rivers Press.

Goleman, D., Boyatzis, R. E., and McKee, A. (2002). *Primal Leadership: Realizing the Power of Emotional Intelligence*. Harvard Business School Press.

Gottman, J. M. (2000). *The Seven Principles for Making Marriage Work: A Practical Guide from the Country's Foremost Relationship Expert.* Three Rivers Press.

Gyaltshen Rinpoche, K. K. (2006). *Transformation of Suffering.* Vajra.

Hackman, J. R. (2002). *Leading Teams: Setting the Stage for Great Performance.* Harvard Business School Press.

Hamachek, D. E. (1978). Psychodynamics of Normal and Neurotic Perfectionism. *Psychology*, 15, 27–33.

Hewitt, P. L., and Flett, G. L. (1991). Perfectionism in the Self and Social Contexts: Conceptualization, Assessment, and Association with Psychopathology. *Journal of Personality and Social Psychology*, 60, 456–470.

Hurley, R. F., and Ryman, J. (2008). Making the Transition from Micromanager to Leader. *Organization Dynamics*, manuscript under review.

James, W. (1890). *Principles of Psychology.* Henry Holt and Co.

James, W. (1988). *William James: Writings 1902–1910.* Library of America.

Kabat-Zinn, J. (1990). *Full Catastrophe Living: The Wisdom of Your Body and Mind to Face Stress, Pain, and Illness.* Delta.

Kabat-Zinn, J. (2003). Mindfulness-Based Interventions in Context: Past, Present, and Future. *Clinical Psychology*, 10(2), 144–156.

Koch, R. (2005). *Living the 80/20 Way: Work Less, Worry Less, Succeed More, Enjoy More.* Nicholas Brealey Publishing.

Kosslyn, S. M. (2005). Reflective Thinking and Mental Imagery: A Perspective on the Development of Posttraumatic Stress Disorder. *Development and Psychopathology*, 17, 851–863.

Kuhn, T. S. (1996). *The Structure of Scientific Revolution.* University of Chicago Press.

Langer, E. J. (1989). *Mindfulness.* Addison-Wesley.

Langer, E. J. (2005). *On Becoming an Artist: Reinventing Yourself Through Mindful Creativity.* Ballantine Books.

Leary, M. R., Tate, E. B., Adams, C. E., Allen, A. B., and Hancock, J. (2007). Self-Compassion and Reactions to Unpleasant Self-Relevant Events: The Implications of Treating Oneself Kindly. *Journal of Personality and Social Psychology*, 92, 887–904.

Levy, B. R. (2003). Mind Matters: Cognitive and Physical Effects of Aging Self-Stereotypes. *Journal of Gerontology*, 58, 203–211.

Levy, B. R., Slade, M. D., Kunkel, S. R., and Kasl, S. V. (2002). Longevity Increased by Positive Self-Perceptions of Aging. *Journal of Personality and Social Psychology*, 83, 261–270.

Locke, E. A., and Latham, G. P. (2002). Building a Practically Useful Theory of Goal Setting and Task Motivation: A 35-Year Odyssey. *American Psychologist*, 57(9) 705–717.

Loehr, J., and Schwartz, T. (2001, January). *The Making of a Corporate Athlete*. Harvard Business Review, 120128.

Loehr, J., and Schwartz, T. (2004). *The Power of Full Engagement: Managing Energy, Not Time, Is the Key to High Performance and Personal Time*. Free Press.

Luthar, S. S., Shoum, K. A., and Brown, P. J. (2006). Extracurricular Involvement Among Affluent Youth: A Scapegoat for "Ubiquitous Achievement Pressures"? *Developmental Psychology*, 42, 583–597.

Lyubomirsky, S. (2007). *The How of Happiness: A Scientific Approach to Getting the Life You Want*. Penguin Press.

Mancini, M. (2007). *Time Management: 24 Techniques to Make Each Minute Count at Work*. McGraw-Hill.

Maslow, A. H. (1993). *The Farther Reaches of Human Nature*. Penguin.

McEvoy, G. M., and Beatty, R. W. (1989). Assessment Centers and Subordinate Appraisals of Managers: A Seven Year Longitudinal Examination of Predictive Validity. *Personnel Psychology*, 42, 37–52.

Mill, J. S. (1974). *The Subjection of Women*. MIT Press.

Montessori, M. (1995). *The Absorbent Mind*. Holt Paperbacks.

Morling, B., and Epstein, S. (1997). Compromises Produced by the Dialectic Between Self-Verification and Self-Enhancement. *Journal of Personality and Social Psychology*, 73, 1268–1283.

Nash, L., and Stevenson, H. (2005). *Just Enough: Tools for Creating Success in Your Work and Life*. Wiley.

Newman, L. S., Duff, K. J., and Baumeister, R. F. (1997). A New Look at Defensive Projection: Thought Suppression, Accessibility, and Biased Person Perception. *Journal of Personality and Social Psychology*, 72, 980–1001.

Nir, D. (2008). *The Negotiational Self: Identifying and Transforming Negotiation Outcomes Within the Self*. Dissertation, School of Business, Hebrew University.

Pacht, A. R. (1984). Reflections on Perfection. *American Psychologist*, 39, 386–390.

Pennebaker, J. W. (1997). *Opening Up*. Guilford Press.

Peterson, C. (2006). *A Primer in Positive Psychology*. Oxford University Press.

Pinker, S. (2006, Spring). The Blank Slate. *The General Psychologist*, 41, 1–8.

Rathunde, K., and Csikszentmihalyi, M. (2005a). The Social Context of Middle School: Teachers, Friends, and Activities in Montessori and Traditional School Environments. *Elementary School Journal*, 106, 59–79.

Rathunde, K., and Csikszentmihalyi, M. (2005b). Middle School Students' Motivation and Quality of Experience: A Comparison of Montessori and Traditional School Environments. *American Journal of Education*, 111, 341–371.

Ray, R. D., Wilhelm, F. H., and Gross, J. J. (2008). All in the Mind's Eye? Anger Rumination and Reappraisal. *Journal of Personality and Social Psychology*, 94, 133–145.

Reivich, K., and Shatte, A. (2003). *The Resilience Factor: 7 Keys to Finding Your Inner Strength and Overcoming Life's Hurdles*. Broadway.

Ricard, M. (2006). *Happiness: A Guide to Developing Life's Most Important Skill*. Little, Brown and Company.

Rogers, C. (1961). *On Becoming a Person: A Therapist's View of Psychotherapy*. Constable.

Scheine, E. H., and Bennis, W. (1965). *Personal and Organizational Change via Group Methods*. Wiley.

Schnarch, D. (1998). *Passionate Marriage: Keeping Love and Intimacy Alive in Committed Relationships*. Owl Books.

Seligman, M. E. P. (1990). *Learned Optimism: How to Change Your Mind and Your Life*. Pocket Books.

Seligman, M. E. P. (2004). *Authentic Happiness: Using the New Positive Psychology to Realize Your Potential for Lasting Fulfillment*. Free Press.

Seligman, M. E. P., Park, N., and Peterson, C. (2005). Positive Psychology Progress: Empirical Validation of Interventions. *American Psychologist*, 60, 410–421.

Siegle, D., and Schuler, P. A. (2000). Perfectionism Differences in Gifted Middle School Students. *Roeper Review*, 23, 39–45.

Smiles, S. (1958). *Self-Help*. John Murray.

Sowell, T. (2007). *A Conflict of Visions: Ideological Origins of Political Struggles*. Basic Books.

Swann, W. B., Pelham, B. W., and Krull, D. S. (1989). Agreeable Fancy or Disagreeable Truth? Reconciling Self-Enhancement and Self-Verification. *Journal of Personality and Social Psychology, 57,* 782–791.

Thoreau, H. D. (2004). *Walden and Civil Disobedience.* Signet Classics.

Tomaka, J., Blascovich, J., Kibler, J., and Ernst, J. M. (1997). Cognitive and Physiological Antecedents of Threat and Challenge Appraisal. *Journal of Personality and Social Psychology, 73,* 63–72.

Wegner, D. M. (1994). *White Bears and Other Unwanted Thoughts: Suppression, Obsession, and the Psychology of Mental Control.* Guilford Press.

Weick, K. E. (1979). *The Social Psychology of Organizing.* McGraw-Hill.

Weick, K. E. (2001). Leadership as the Legitimation of Doubt. In W. Bennis, G. M. Spreitzer, and T. Cummings (eds.), *The Future of Leadership: Today's Top Thinkers on Leadership Speak to the Next Generation,* 91–102. Jossey-Bass.

Wenzlaff, R. M., and Wegner, D. M. (2000). Thought Suppression. *Annual Review of Psychology, 51,* 59–91.

Williams, M. G., Teasdale, J. D., Segal, Z. V., and Kabat-Zinn, J. (2007). *The Mindful Way Through Depression: Freeing Yourself from Chronic Unhappiness.* Guilford Press.

Wilson, E. G. (2008). *Against Happiness: In Praise of Melancholy.* Farrar, Straus, and Giroux.

Winnicott, D. W. (1982). *Playing and Reality.* Routledge.

Winnicott, D. W. (1990). *Home Is Where We Start From: Essays by a Psychoanalyst.* Norton & Company.

Worden, J. W. (2008). *Grief Counseling and Grief Therapy: A Handbook for the Mental Health Practitioner, Fourth Edition.* Springer Publishing Company.

Yerkes, R. M., and Dodson, J. D. (1908). The Relation of Strength of Stimulus to Rapidity of Habit-Formation. *Journal of Comparative Neurology and Psychology, 18,* 459–482.

# Index